SHATTERING MASKS

By

Laura Beth Taylor

sophia sojourn

Cover design by Laura Beth

Back cover photo by Song Spicer, Songbird Photography

Printed by Create Space, Charleston, SC

ISBN 978-0692773536

For more information and ordering: www.sophiasojourn.com

While writing in a journal that I have had since high school, I recently re-read the inscription from the friend who gave it to me:

Bryan,

Over the past few months you have shown me so much through your writing. Many of your thoughts are "deep", provoking anyone who reads them to <u>listen</u> to what you are saying. Thank you for sharing some of those thoughts with me. I hope that you will continue to share them with me, but I also believe that your thoughts should be bound together for a total meaning rather than sent in pieces to all ends of the earth. For this reason I give you this book - for your deep thoughts. Your writing is incredible + God has touched it in many ways. May this book inspire you to take your wonderful thoughts to paper more often. One day, I hope to be able to have you share this book with me to try to understand you even better. Until then, all my love + your deepest thoughts —

In God's love,
Kate

To all the teachers, friends, relatives and mentors who have encouraged me, as Kate did, to capture my thoughts and pursue my writing, thank you. It's the only place in the book my old name appears; please consider it my way of honoring you and the investment you made in me.

In memory of those whose stories ended before their time and dedicated to those living on the fringes or in the margins; You are my motivation. You are my tribe.

Special thanks to...

My family: Graydon, Ella, Mea, Josh and Lyndon...
You are more loved than you can know.

Moms and Dad...
You put the "un" in unconditional love.

Serenitarians...
You all happened, and you just keep happening!
(and what a coincidence, it was right when I needed you.)

Susan H...
Your patience, encouragement and ability to help me see beyond my own nose are uncanny.

Kat...
You bring new meaning and depth to the concepts of inspiration and friendship.

Tammy...
Few people possess the ability to push me out of my comfort zone into great new places. I'm glad you do!

M...
I wouldn't trade the years for anything; you are the mom our kids need and a blessing to so many.

Susan D...
You are teaching me what it means to "be gentle with me."

Dr. Sara &Dr. Cara...
You were among the first to believe in me and your persistence has paid off.

Morning Song

Grace in the morning, Lord, when I start to rise;
Grace enough to lift my head
And look into your eyes.
For it's only when I'm touched by grace,
I can look into your holy face
And be about the work you'd have me do.
Grace in the morning, Lord that I might be like you.

Love in the morning, Lord, to see me through the day.
Love enough to share with those
I meet along the way
For it's only when they see your love
That they'll see what I'm made of;
Lord your love has made my life brand new.
Love in the morning, Lord that I might be like you.

Hope in the morning, Lord, for all the days to come.
Hope in the resurrection
Your return and the kingdom come.
For it's only in the hope you give
That I'm free to truly live
And there's noting more that I would rather do
Hope in the morning, Lord that I might be like you.

(circa 1994 – a rare peak from behind the masks)

Table of Contents

Preface

Sometime in the middle of August 2015, I started to slide into an intense depressive state. I recognized it when I saw it. I had been there before. But this time it didn't concern me. I embraced it for what it was: a cycle of my life, simply part of the adventure that is my existence. Toward the end of that month, I was having dinner with a friend and the subject of my writing came to the conversation. I had been toying with different ideas for writing a book, but I could not settle on exactly what the book needed to be about. I have several passions. My life is not lacking in interesting things to share. But what was my purpose in writing?

The conversation that night took several twists and turns and I found myself in a wonderfully emotional frame of mind. It was the first time that I could remember being in that deep of a state of depression *and* feeling safe enough to allow emotions that intense to carry on unchecked. The conversation kept going in my mind long after the dinner was over. And that's when it hit me: the purpose of the book was the conversation. The initial draft was done in the next thirty days. There was a great deal of editing to be done, but once it started rolling, I couldn't have stopped writing if I had wanted to.

There are many conversations that need to be happening around dinner tables, boardrooms, pastor's offices, school counselor's desks, therapist's couches, and any number of other spots where thought, personality, and culture collide. These are conversations about the more challenging things life throws at us — like the depression I just weathered, questions regarding our identity, and challenges to our faith. My hope is that the thoughts and stories I share on these pages serve that purpose.

One key to any good conversation is some sort of common understanding between both sides that gives context to the ideas that are being expressed. As I revisited and adjusted everything from my faith to my gender expression in the last few years, I struggled to find that unifying framework that provided context for these challenging concepts. I finally found the beginnings of a cohesive conceptualization/framework in an article that Mom sent me about gender dysphoria (the clinical term for the experience of many transgender people) by Dr. Mark Yarhouse.

Dr. Yarhouse is a professor of psychology at Regent University in Virginia Beach, Virginia. Though there are many points of contention I have with his conclusions and approaches to LGBTQ people, the article and his book *Understanding Gender Dysphoria* were a significant catalyst for conversation between my parents and me. In these publications, Yarhouse describes three lenses through which he has observed Christians looking at gender identity: "integrity," "disability," and "diversity."

While I'm not totally on board with these particular labels and their implications, they served as a beginning point for a grounded framework. I set my mind to creating my own version of these lenses; a model that could apply to many other areas where personal identity and religious or cultural thought intermingle. I have presented that model here in its early form. I am certain it will evolve as my own journey progresses, and in the meantime I hope it will provide a helpful frame of reference for you as you read this book.

When you encounter a particular thought or idea that rubs you the wrong way, ask yourself through which lens are you viewing the subject. In a sense, I am inviting you to examine potential biases. Then, if you are willing, step back and look at the issue again through one of the other lenses. It may be more of a challenge than you are ready for, trying on various lenses. In that case, try looking somewhere in between them. (And if after all that you still find yourself offended, be sure and read the bonus section at the end of the book, "The Defensive Nature of Being Offended.")

So here are my three lenses:

Dichotomy

This is a red light. The proverbial buck stops here. Looking through this lens, one sees things as either right or wrong, black or white. The decision is usually based on some religious or culturally accepted standard of "normal." Adherents to this lens have a strong sense of moral and/or spiritual conviction and are often rather passionate about their position on a specific topic. This conviction, often based on religious texts such as the Bible, is presented in such a way that there can be little room for flexibility of thought and perspective. Those who wear these glasses are sometimes so loyal to the way in which they interpret scripture that they are decidedly invested in a more literal interpretation and perceived moral grounding through which they respond to various topics. They are informed by this black and white perspective, creating firm judgments on issues with great moral conviction.

Deferment.

This is a caution light. Those with this perspective still operate within the context of a religious or cultural standard but they are willing to accept that certain ideas and life experiences may arise that fail to fit in the moral boxes they have adopted. This dissonance gives way to a willingness to defer judgment. The deferment lens allows more flexibility than the dichotomy lens, while maintaining certain moral or religious boundaries.

From many Christians' viewpoints, anything that draws people away from the initial intent of "God's created order" (or more accurately, their interpretation of that order) could be considered outside of "normal." Integrating these instances into everyday life presents ideological hardships. By deferring any moral decision, one can maintain the basic integrity of those moral boundaries without discrediting or disassociating with anyone that falls outside them for any reason.

Diversity.

This is a green light. By far the most flexible of the three, this lens celebrates anything and everything that makes a person unique. It can be viewed within the context of a religious or cultural code, but does not particularly require one. As Dr. Yarhouse points out, people who use this lens usually fall into one of two categories. The first sub-lens is "extreme-diversity." For those who see others strictly through this lens, there are few if any versions of humanity for which they will not make room in their worldview. A less extreme interpretation of this lens celebrates the diversity and uniqueness while striving for some balance with the other lenses. Looking at the world in the context of "moderate-diversity" will allow the freedom to question certain perspectives while maintaining an overarching principle of acceptance and celebration.

I hope this helps you get more out of the conversation that's about to happen. The way we see other people, especially the way we see ourselves, will ultimately define the way we live out particular concepts such as love and grace.

Introduction

---

mask: noun 1) a full or partial covering of the face worn to conceal one's identity; 2) anything that disguises or conceals, offers pretense[1] She used her intellect, strength, creativity and faith as a mask for the pain she felt.

---

[1] Retrieved from www.dictionary.com, July 17, 2016

In January 2015, I responded to the encouragement of a friend and started writing. I journaled, wrote letters, and eventually captured my thoughts and stories in a blog. "Sophia Sojourn," my "journey into wisdom," has proven to be a great outlet for my creativity and musings. One morning, as I was watching the sun come up and contemplating life, I simply wrote, "It's a new day and I'm learning that . . . ." I typed out the thought, put it on a picture of the sunrise that I snapped with my iPhone that morning, and published it on the blog — resisting the urge to add any commentary or explanation. The meme could speak for itself, relaying whatever message the reader needed to hear. It became a theme for the blog.

As time pressed on, my "New Day" thoughts came to represent life lessons which were helping me move forward rather than wallowing in the moment, allowing hurts and fears to linger. Over the next few months, more and more people were encouraging me to tell more of my story. I looked again at the growing collection of New Day memes and it occurred to me, "These lessons *are* telling my story." All I needed to do was allow a little more vulnerability, share more about what was going on in my heart and mind at the time of each epiphany, and tell the story in a relatable text.

"Relatable" seemed like a tall order. My life felt too complicated to be highly relatable. On the other hand, I've never met anyone who calmly stated, "My life is pleasantly uncomplicated." If those people exist, their lives are likely still that way because they have cleverly avoided meeting people like me. I have met people who are so overwhelmed with their life circumstances that they are afraid to make any changes. I've also known people who are so bored with their lives that they make rash decisions in order to make rapid changes. I've been both of those people and the pages ahead will provide more depth to the complications of life in my shoes.

To put these essays and stories in context, allow me to introduce myself a bit more thoroughly. I'll do that using some common labels, even though they don't all totally fit.

- I identify as Christian, but please don't walk away if you don't. This is not intended to be a "Christian" book. I'll share about my faith journey and how I've found myself in a season of deconstructing and rebuilding my belief system. Regardless of what you believe, I'd like to think you could relate to my (mis)adventures in your own journey.

- I am a Transwoman. By that, I mean simply that my biological sex was determined to be male at birth, but socially and psychologically I identify more strongly as a woman. In my case there are also medical conditions that give me the label "intersex." If you have doubts or uncertainty about gender identity (mine or anyone else's), please stick around and learn more about that piece of my journey.

- I am a student. Sometimes this is a formality as I venture back into a college setting, but it is always a reality as I read, listen, and learn from whomever, whenever, wherever I am able. It's as much a part of who I am as eating and breathing.

- I am a parent and a grandparent. I am also recently divorced (something that will be discussed in the upcoming stories). I have also been a son, now a daughter to two loving and compassionate parents and I am the younger sibling to a sister who was my best friend through much of our growing up years. I have nieces and nephews, a brother-in-law, and a sister-in-law. If you happen to be single or still happily married, don't worry: this is not a book about marriage or divorce.

- I am a professional. I hold an interdisciplinary degree in mass communications and Christian ministry. I have worked for not-for-profits, churches, large corporations and small start-up companies. I spent many of my younger years in the music industry doing studio work, producing events and managing tours for Christian musicians. However, as you may have guessed, this is not a book about career advice or mapping the road to professional satisfaction.

- I have struggles. Don't we all? I wrestle with major depressive disorder, anxiety, and post-traumatic stress disorder (PTSD) in addition to all the other liabilities of being human.

And that's what the book is about: *me.* But this is the "me" that can only be found when you look *between* the labels and *beyond* the cultural identities.

The chapters don't cover my life in chronological order. For those suffering from obsessive-compulsive disorder, I am deeply sorry. Perhaps someday I'll create a timeline for you. This is not intended to be a memoir, telling my life story from the beginning.

My hope is that you find something specific that my story has to offer you, like so many sunrises have spoken to me in recent months. And at the end of the day, I hope you are encouraged to live a more genuine, authentic life.

It's time to shatter the masks.

Chapter 1:
The Mask of Remembering

"It's a new day, and I'm learning that memories are not ghosts that haunt us, they are the threads of a tapestry reminding us how we became who we are."

Memories are the gift we are given to hold on to things to which words and pictures could never do justice. My life is full of them. Many of them make my eyes misty with fondness for the sweet moments they represent; many of them cause me to lie awake at night fearing the visions with which they invade my dreams.

All of them weave together to make "me." The good, the bad, and the ever-so-slightly edgy all knitted tightly into my being as they refine my character and shape my view of the world around me. My intention in writing this book is to share just a few of them; and in sharing them, break free of the masks they represent in my life. The memories I'll be sharing are some of the more relevant moments that convey the major parts of my story.

I could start where most life stories start. I was born in California. It was 1972 . . . but this isn't my whole life story, and besides, I don't have a memory of being born, at least not an accurate memory as you will discover. Let me start with something I do remember and then work my way on from there.

Here we go, again

The ritual is familiar to every military brat. Every two to three years, the family gathered around the kitchen table or perhaps in the living room. In our case, "family" meant Dad, Moms (I'm not exactly sure why we call her "Moms," but my sister started it and it works for us), Kayla, and myself, the little brother. The purpose of these meetings was never really a mystery: Dad had new orders. It was time to pack up and go again.

In our house, relocating was usually met with excitement and a sense of adventure. Sure we were leaving friends, church, and a surrounding where we were comfortable, but we had known all along this day would come; and consequently, we hadn't ever let ourselves become too comfortable. There were usually tears at good-byes and address books were updated (address book = analog contacts app), but once we were on the road, it was all about looking forward.

I was an 11-year-old boy in the summer of 1983. Kayla was two years older and these moving adventures usually helped create a pretty tight bond between the two of us. The current escapade had us rolling, flying, and floating from Virginia Beach, Virginia, to Roosevelt Roads, Puerto Rico. Since these trips usually allowed a fair amount of time, our tradition was to make a vacation out of them. That summer we headed north and west before heading south. We visited family in Massachusetts, South Dakota, Colorado, and New Mexico. We saw Niagara Falls, rode the Chi-Cheemaun Ferry across the Great Lakes, and took in the awesome sights of Mount Rushmore and Devil's Tower. It was a summer of memories — *mostly* great memories.

And then this . . .

We had an extended stay hotel in Athens, Georgia, where Dad was attending a class at the Naval Supply School. While we were there, all of our household belongings were neatly packed in shipping crates and sitting in a warehouse in San Juan awaiting our arrival. I really don't recall whether it was morning or afternoon. It was warm out, but it was summer in the south — it could have been any time. I don't remember if the skies were cloudy or clear. I don't remember if the sun was shining or if it was raining. I do remember a sinking feeling in my stomach when Kayla and I overheard a conversation that had Moms in tears.

"Even all my pots and pans" was the phrase that resounds in my mind. Dad had just told her that the warehouse that stored nearly all our material possessions had burned to the ground. There was speculation of arson, with some blame passed on to union labor. In the end it really didn't matter. Ashes are ashes, no matter the source of the spark.

Before long the news was delivered directly to the two of us. No longer needing to eavesdrop, we began the process of mourning our stuff. My coin collection, my train set, my leather working tools. I thought of the dollhouse that Dad had custom-built for my sister. In addition to pots and pans, Moms was grieving the loss of pictures and family heirlooms. From that moment on, "stuff" has had a new, less prominent place in my life. It was amazing how quickly we reacquired plenty of it again, but I don't think I have been attached to a "thing" in the same way since that day.

The days ahead were packed with inspiring stories of people stepping up to help us recover from this tragedy. The demands of military life create a tight community. News of the fire and the eleven families it victimized had reached the base. Military personnel and other families were mobilizing resources before we ever landed on the island. We took a shopping trip back to the states to replace what we could. Our church community back in Virginia rallied around us and helped with places to stay, vehicles to use, and other details that a massive shopping trip would present. Dad didn't want the house to look like it fell out of the pages of a catalog, so he introduced Kayla and me to the grand tradition of estate sale shopping. Something resembling a familiar home soon took shape.

Rethinking Christmas

As I remember it, Christmas of 1983 was a particular challenge. In addition to forcefully foregoing our traditional live tree (a natural, yet unfortunate casualty of living in the tropics), I became aware of a particularly significant loss from the fire. Dad had collected Christmas ornaments from his deployments around the world. Pulling them out of the boxes every year was always a meaningful time for us to hear the stories and bond around those memories. Our tree that year taught me that bonding and memories have special ways of reinventing themselves.

I'm not sure whose idea it was (I know it wasn't mine), but I remember putting it into action. We headed out to Humacao Beach on the southeast side of Puerto Rico. We had been told that this was a wonderful spot to gather sand dollars from the ocean floor. We weren't disappointed. We walked along in water as high as my chest, felt the live sand dollars with our feet, dove down, and picked them up by the handful. Within a short amount of time, the five of us admired over a hundred beautiful sand dollars (and there were still thousands more we left behind).

What we do for family

You may have noticed I said "five" of us. In addition to Dad, Moms, Kayla, and myself, my maternal grandmother (Grandma Leslie) had come to live with us during our stay in the Caribbean. She ended up staying a lot longer, but that's another story. She had a fun and adventurous personality and was usually willing to give most anything new a try, including hunting for sand dollars.

However, there was a problem: to use her own word, Grandma was a little "fluffy." Whenever she waded with her fluffiness into the salty ocean water of the Caribbean, it was difficult for her to dive down to retrieve the sand dollars off the seabed. Floating and relaxing came quite easy; diving to the bottom was a problem. She and Dad worked out a solution. When she had found some sand dollars with her feet and was ready to collect them, she called him over, stuck her face in the water and he pushed her down by her back. He would hold her down until she had had enough time to pick up a few of the treasures.

For years to come he described this as the best "mother-in-law therapy" ever. She loved to tell the story and over the years her respect for my dad grew.

Trimming the tree

We carefully cleaned, bleached, and coated the sand dollars with a solution of water and glue and then spread them out to dry under the tropical sun. We placed our newly purchased artificial spruce tree in the living room, right in front of a window where we could see the palm trees waving in the background. Next came strings of over 500 white lights draped across the tree's blue branches. Finally, we positioned the bright white sand dollars around the tree, each tied delicately with a thin, red ribbon.

Of all our Christmas trees before and since, I can't recall a more stunning tree. In my preteen mind, it was a simple declaration of starting over, with family at the center of our path forward. We soon began to collect new ornaments and our tree once again took on a life of its own. The tree of '83, however, was simple and clean. It didn't need "stuff" to make it beautiful.

Moving forward

As I mentioned, stuff seemed to collect quickly and eventually "BF" (before fire) and "AF" (after fire) belongings blended together. For years it seemed we would go looking for something and have to stop and ask ourselves if it was purchased BF or AF. Three years later, we were once again gathered at the kitchen table and presented with a new adventure. This one took us back to Virginia along with a shipment of household goods that still managed to max out our weight limit.

Shattering Masks

Chapter 2:
The Mask of Thick Skin

---

*"I've dealt with a great deal of
humiliation in my life, but it's a new
day and I'm learning that one does not
have to be humiliated to be humble.
Humility is a virtue;
humiliation is a cancer."*

There was more to our time in Puerto Rico than sand dollars and sandy beaches. Granted, the ability to have a beach party for my birthday in the middle of February was a lovely perk, as was the school bus that dropped us off at either the golf course or the stables every day. There were tennis courts, pools, a bowling alley, a pizza parlor — most all within a decent bike ride of home. However I was a pre-adolescent boy and all the tropical bliss of the islands can't hold off the physical or social challenges of this stage of life. I was concurrently learning the need for humility in the face of privilege and the sting of humiliation. I carried the growth and the scars from both lessons deep into my adult years.

Privilege that might have been

Since I affirmed my gender identity a few years ago, I have frequently been asked about the loss of my male privilege. In fact, I have been told my life was brimming with privilege. I was a white, Christian, educated, heterosexual male of average height and weight living in the "Bible belt." According to many sociologists' models, I was at the top of the social food chain. While I was never specifically aware of most of those unearned advantages, the reality of our society is that many of us have silent privileges we enjoy simply as a result of the skin, bodies, and families we are born into. It's true I may have enjoyed certain "male privileges" — for example when I took my car into the shop to get it worked on.

I recently tested this privilege when shopping for new tires. I was still early in the transition process and had more flexibility to present either masculine or feminine. I visited one location of a major tire chain store wearing khaki capris, a cute top and sparkly earrings. After a moment in line, I told the middle-aged gentleman at the check-in counter I needed two new tires. After inspecting the vehicle, he "mansplained" to me that I actually needed four tires and that based on the type of vehicle, I was only given two options, both of which were the most expensive in the their line. I wish I could say I was surprised, but this was the exact experience that had been explained to me by nearly every cis-woman with whom I'd ever discussed the topic. I wasn't done though. I went to a second store presenting as masculine as I could (no jewelry, jeans and a loose button down shirt, hair pulled back, etc.). I told the staff at this store the exact same thing: I need two new tires. The only suggestion that was made was to rotate the tires to allow the remaining two to wear evenly.

To test another variable, I visited a third store presenting as myself again, but this time in addition to telling the staff I needed two new tires, I also told them that I had already measured the tread and knew they would pass inspection. I told them very specifically that I only needed a road tread with a particular mileage range. I didn't mention the rotation. They never mentioned the four tires. The technician did suggest the rotation and, in addition to showing me the tires I asked about, also suggested a slight upgrade that cost only a little extra.

My takeaway from this very unscientific experiment is not only that male privilege exists, but also that in order to overcome it, women need to be extra diligent in preparing themselves for these types of situations. The lesson reiterated the fact that I need to teach my daughters as much about cars and their maintenance as I do my son. I could, and often do, speak to the need for better education of men (boys) regarding how they respect women — something that would be a valuable addition to our culture in general. The unfortunate reality is that, in my opinion, we are several generations from seeing any sort of reversal in these trends. We need to deal with the reality of the here and the now.

One thing that kept my sense of privilege at bay was that it always felt like there was someone else with more of it. Yes, I was seeing the benefit of male privilege, but for the most part it always seemed that other men in my life were better at doing "man" than I was. From my perspective, men around me were faster, stronger, more bold, better spoken, better with money, better leaders, better fathers. or better husbands. That nagging feeling of being second rate, even within the context of a particular "in group" such as a church leadership team, ultimately prevented me from experiencing, let alone asserting, any specific privilege.

Sticks and stones…

The almost-but-not-quite belief has deep roots in some of my earliest social memories. In my own mind I was OK at most everything, but not good at anything. There wasn't anywhere I stood out to the point that I felt like I was really on my home turf. In hindsight, I did have arenas in my life that fit that description: I was a good horseback rider, I was a good musician, I was a good writer. Something I have observed is that as kids we tend to not recognize the moments of success. We focus on shortcomings, specifically as our peers generously point them out to us.

I'll never forget sitting in a fourth grade classroom and having to cross from one side of the room to the other when we switched from history and reading to science and math. For the former I was in the top of the class and sat with those who were in the same group. For the latter, I was — well — not near the top of the class and I sat with other kids who were "more my speed" in those disciplines. As I gathered my assorted papers and pencils and stood up to make the daily trek to "slowville," "Straight-A Jay" looked at me and said,

"There goes the faggot." He laughed. I don't remember if anyone else did or not, but I recall thinking he was amused with himself.

I don't remember responding, mostly because I didn't know what the word "faggot" meant. After school, I looked it up to discover in my 1980-something dictionary that a faggot was "a bundle of sticks." I assumed for years that he was calling me skinny — which was fitting for my slender physique. It wasn't until later events caused me to question everything in my past that I connected the dots between his slur and what he may have thought about my gender presentation. Was he saying I was too girly because I was skinny? Was he saying I looked like someone who should be attracted to other boys?

Another moment seared into my memory happened on a middle school soccer field. I was good enough to make the team, even strong enough to make the starting lineup. In my mind, it wasn't my soccer skills, but rather my sense of enthusiasm that landed me on the team. (It was years before I realized the value of that character trait.) I wasn't alone in questioning the coach's judgment for assigning me to the first string. On a particularly warm practice day as I was sweating more than usual, my game was off and I was performing a little less than "OK." One of my teammates yelled, "Pass it to 'toast,' see if we can burn him." The name stuck. I was branded as "Toast" the remainder of the soccer season. It was especially amusing when I showed up at practice after recently getting a haircut. It wasn't just any haircut, either. I went from a classic 1980's surfer's wave to a high-and-tight military cut.

"Look, Toast got scraped." They laughed. I laughed; at least on the outside.

There were many other profound incidents of bullying that caused me to doubt my sexual orientation, question my gender identity, and reconsider my place in society. Other people's thoughts and perspectives mold how we relate to them. Without even realizing it, I was sewing the cruel names and comments into the very fibers of my identity, knitting my depression and anxiety more deeply into my being. The negativity somehow manages to overshadow any number of "way to go" and "I'm proud of you" affirmations from teachers, coaches, and parents. Good grades or awards and trophies make less of an impact than cruel words from unqualified sources. They unfairly defined me regardless of their inaccuracy or irrelevance.

Fear's residual impact

My least favorite question these days is "How's the job search?" The only good job search is the search that is over. Until then, job hunters faced with that question are compelled to lie or disclose "leads" while minimizing the ever-climbing stack of rejections.

"I've got some good leads."

"I think the market is picking up."

"I had a good feeling about a conversation I had yesterday."

Let's face it, until the answer is, "I got a paycheck yesterday," the rest are mere platitudes. I appreciate the thoughts and concern, just be prepared for a grim and frustrating facial expression should I feel less than compelled to candy coat my response with optimistic rhetoric.

Over the past several months, I've been on a job hunt. It's not a new activity for me. I've been on many of them over the past several years. But as I've navigated the gender transition and the shifts in perceived and experienced privileges, I've become more and more aware of the doubts implanted in my mind years ago. Am I good enough for this job? Why would they want me? What do I really have to offer? The questions undermine any response that I receive from a job prospect.

Humiliations galore!

The taunts of our peers, rejection — in the job market or anywhere else — all aspire toward one master sensation: humiliation. As with so many lessons of life, so many things might have been different had I learned this earlier, but I eventually figured out the crucial difference between *humility* and *humiliation*. The ability to distinguish them earlier might have yielded healthier boundaries and more assertive behavior on my part. The notion of humility that Christ shows us — being willing to be less than we really are for the sake of others — is vastly different from the humiliation that is reinforced by our culture and, sadly, much of the church. The church's message of "you are less" unfortunately robbed me of the opportunity to willingly become less. Over time, humiliation stifled true humility; I'm only now learning to live in the light of that truth.

Recognizing humiliation as the cancer it is seemed like a good place to start the process of reshaping my image of me.

Chapter 3:

The Mask of Innocence

"For most of my life, I've valued people because I needed them in order to see value in myself. It's a new day and I'm learning that only in seeing the value in myself can I truly see the value in other people."

Despite the occasional taunting, Puerto Rico was a blissful paradise. As is all too often the case with adolescents, my peers and I basked in the warm glow of that paradise while at the same time frequently complaining about our existence. We would swim year round, but it was constantly humid. We had magical outdoor, rainforest-like spaces, but the bugs were terrible. We could walk to a movie theater, but our selection was usually about six months behind the mainland. Most of us wanted our free time there to last forever, but concurrently couldn't wait to "get off this rock and back to the States."

Leaving the island with its warm breezes, incredible sunsets, and salty ocean air became symbolic of leaving behind a more innocent life. But innocence lasts for only a season, and the sun was about to set on that season of my life. I wouldn't be able to make sense of what was to happen for another decade or two. Sometimes the right time and the right people in our lives help us finally step forward.

Surrendering identity

I'll never forget the first time I drove by a military base after dutifully surrendering my dependent ID card. Life on the base had been safe, just like playing tag as a kid: if you make it back to base you're home free. The base was familiar, no matter where in the world I happened to find it. There was a commissary, an Exchange or PX (think Wal-Mart or Target), and usually a golf course or a movie theater. For my first 21 years, as long as I was in school, I could drive, walk, or ride my bike up to the gate, pull out my ID, show it to the marine or soldier standing guard duty, and they would grant me permission to pass. Relinquishing that privilege and driving by the gate knowing that I couldn't get past the guardhouse was a spotlight shining on my own coming of age. I was growing out of identifying as a "dependent" and into an identity that was all my own.

Frankly, it scared the crap out of me. I had no clue who I was, no concept of my own identity. It would take a long time for me to figure that out and in the meantime, I floundered.

The balance of self and others

I suffer from chronic people pleasing. On the surface, my ability to adapt might appear to be a positive quality — after all, who doesn't want to be pleased? In my heart I always questioned whether people simply loved to have me around because I would do whatever it took to make sure the relationship remained undamaged and completely intact or if they really valued my company. It made sense to me at the time. It's what I thought serving people was all about: making it about them all the time and never being "selfish" with what I wanted, or even needed. What an impossible paradigm to maintain. Eventually my own needs always arose and instead of dealing with them directly, I became frustrated and angry and lashed out at those closest to me. The result was a vicious cycle that took a great deal of soul-searching to break.

I didn't really realize this cycle was even an issue until it was brought to my attention that somewhere along the way, I had wandered off the path toward discovering my own identity. I had become such a skilled chameleon that I had no idea of who I authentically was when all else was stripped away, when the lights went off at night and there was nothing left in the darkness but the silence, my own thoughts, and God as I understood God. *Who was I?* What motivated me? What brought me pleasure? What really bothered me? What are my pet peeves? But I certainly didn't take the time to ask these questions. That would be *selfish*.

Over the years, as I worked through my own identity conflicts, I began to examine where the pattern began. At what point did I start to make less of myself and more of others, not out of genuine humility, but out of self-preservation? More specifically, when did I lose the balance and allow myself to be defined by what everyone else thought I should be and deny myself my own identity? A possible explanation occurred to me when I finally mustered the courage to invite someone to peer behind the mask.

Accepting PTSD

Sometime in 2006, I finally decided I needed to return to a therapist to sort out some personal struggles. I had been married to "M" for eight years and to say our marriage was unhealthy would be a gross understatement.

Since my senior year of high school I had been experiencing extreme abdominal pain that, despite countless scans and unspeakable poking and prodding, remained undiagnosed.

I wasn't sleeping well.

My discomfort with my gender identity was brewing, very real to me but unspoken and beneath the surface of my everyday existence. I felt irritable and depressed practically all the time.

We had a new baby girl at home and M was experiencing extreme postpartum depression. Not recognizing the depth and complexity of her sadness, I failed to respond to her in a way that could have promoted healing and recovery.

All of these personal factors combined made relating to each other in a productive, emotionally healthy way extremely difficult. At times it felt impossible. I ignored all the swelling emotions that sought to swallow me and internalized the "blame" for where our relationship had devolved. Clearly everything was my fault.

I sought help from the counselor with high expectations for him to evaluate me and assign some "homework" to resolve my issues. I also expected him to be shocked and somewhat appalled when I disclosed my more intimate personal experiences, including dreaming and waking thoughts of feminization, difficulty with sexual intimacy and other complicated physical symptoms. He actually glossed right over my self-declared shockers and focused his attention on a painful experience from my past that I had disclosed on his intake form.

"Has anyone ever told you that you may be experiencing some levels of complex PTSD?"

The question struck me from left field. My initial reaction was to deny it. Of course this wasn't true. Could this be true? What was he talking about? Having been raised in a military family, I hold deep respect for those who have served our country and put themselves in harm's way. Post Traumatic Stress Disorder (PTSD) was for combat veterans. I declared to him, and myself, that I had not *earned* PTSD.

The moment I began to lose "me"

And about that intake form. What had I written that captured his attention?

The transition from middle to high school is an exciting and challenging time of life. For me, that pivotal evolution came in 1986. It was the year of the Space Shuttle Challenger tragedy, the year Whitney Houston's "The Greatest Love of All" graced the radio waves, and the year our family was transplanted from Puerto Rico to Williamsburg, Virginia. I liked a lot of things about moving to new places. None of the foolishness of middle school would follow me to high school. I looked forward to establishing all new levels of embarrassing moments and crazy antics over the next four years. I planned to take my new school by storm. I felt confident, on top of my game, and ready to kick ass and take names.

Just as when we moved to Puerto Rico, this adventure was accompanied by a trip around the country. We took our time driving from place to place, often roaming off the beaten path to visit family and friends. That particular summer happened to coincide with a family reunion that occurred roughly every four years. Come August, we found ourselves in a camp/resort at the foot of the beautiful Collegiate Peaks in northern Colorado.

Tradition dictated that the older male cousins crash together in one of the suites. These were not merely my first cousins, who I knew rather well, but included more distant cousins who weren't as familiar to me. We ranged in age from 14 (me) to 19 or 20. Early the second evening of the reunion as we sat in the suite awkwardly sharing stories and mindlessly watching something on the television, one of the older cousins asked me to walk with him to get some ice. As we approached the vending machines, he hit me with a question I had never been asked directly.

"Are you gay?"

I had to catch my breath. Why would he even ask me this? I had been raised to *believe exactly what the Bible appears to say*: being gay was a sin. Ours was a "Christian" family. Surely no one here would go against what the Bible "clearly" teaches. I composed myself and mustered an answer.

"No!" Why would he ask me that?

"Oh. Well I am. Kind of, sort of gay."

"Oh." Why would he tell me that?

What just happened? My stunned confusion at the conversation that just took place made the cold ice bucket in my hands seem like part of another dimension. Nothing could have prepared me for what happened next.

I was startled awake in the middle of the night to find him on top of me. For what seemed like an eternity, his actions planted memories in my mind and feelings in my soul that proved to be some of the most terrifying of my life. In those timeless moments, fear froze both my muscles and my voice. I could neither resist nor cry out for help. I was trapped by both his physical presence and my own response to the ensuing terror. Even as I lay there lifeless, I began to wonder, *what does this mean about me?* Was something changing? What was he taking from me? Would I feel this sense of helplessness for the rest of my life? There was no way to answer those questions; I had no sense of past or future. The only reality I knew was the uncertainty of the moment; I was consumed with guilt that I couldn't explain. As my body responded to his actions, there was a physical draining that felt like my life and soul were slipping away from me. Eventually I became aware that he was pulling the sheets out from beneath me. Then, I was aware of tears. They were down to my chin, but I had not been aware of them until that moment. Tears from an empty place as I curled into the corner of the futon, hoping with all hopes to just melt into its cushion and disappear from sight.

To say it was a loss of innocence would be a gross understatement; it was the shredding of a world that was simple and straightforward. Almost immediately, "complexity" became the template for nearly every thought I attempted to sort in my mind. Right and wrong blurred. Physical love and natural reactions to intimacy became tainted with confusion and guilt. Latent, passing thoughts about my gender and sexuality still haunted my sleep. My vision of the world around me was clouded by a severely distorted lens. For decades, I lived with the false assumption that being gay and being a predator were one and the same.

We finished that trip to Colorado forging our way back to Virginia. En route, we picked up two horses that were being retired off of a ranch and we bought a trailer to haul them east with us. My grandfather, Poppy, made the trip with us and I recall spending countless hours with him in his truck staring at the horses tails as we traveled the long highways across the Eastern plains. Though he loved to tell stories and was known as a cowboy poet, he was often a man of few words. He lacked any compulsion to fill the silence with needless chatter. My mind still reeling from the reunion, the silence reinforced the death that was taking place inside my head. The rhythm of the road as it passed under the tires was in sync with the throbbing in my wrists, still slightly bruised from being held down. Thoughts and images replayed like a highlight reel from hell, planting seeds for distortions that would persist for years, if not for the rest of my life. *There is something about me that told him this was OK. I must be broken and flawed. Does this mean I'm gay now? What if someone finds out?* I couldn't live with the outcomes and answers to these thoughts and questions, so I let that part of me die. This living death paved the way for my first real mask.

The Masking

We spent the remainder of the summer settling into our new home and community. I don't recall many specific memories of those days, at least not of what was happening in the world around me. What I do remember is questioning everything I believed about myself. *Why did this happen? Was it something about me? What did it mean about me?* So much for taking my school by storm; much of my freshman year of high school is a blur. I became reclusive, spending most of my time alone in my room, accompanied only by my guitar.

Kayla had become active in the local chapter of Young Life, an organization focused on Christian discipleship among high school students. She shared her concern about my shift in behavior with a few of the adult leaders. That winter a couple of the leaders came up to my room and knocked on the door to invite me on a retreat where they needed me to play guitar. As it turns out, I was one of six people playing the guitar that weekend. They may not have exactly *needed* me to play, but they knew *I* needed to play. Their ruse was effective in getting me out of my room and reengaging with people.

On that retreat I began to discover my emerging talent of blending in with the crowd. I picked up on a distinct culture among the members of Young Life, which I almost immediately emulated. They were spiritual, with a low-key attitude. They were intensely focused both on having fun and diving headfirst into understanding the Bible and how to apply it to their lives. Those who understood that, and were able to articulate the best thoughts and offer the best ways to use the chapters and verses we studied, earned the respect of the inner circle. I quickly realized I had the ability to offer insights that captured their attention. I discovered a confidence that came from adopting those behaviors. This revelation proved to be a refreshing contrast to being locked away in my room wrestling with my own reality. I had found my new public persona. This was now my identity. *I get it. I am clear on who I am and who this safe, Christian culture needs me to be.* Maybe I could take my school by storm after all.

After the retreat, I continued to refine my keen ability to fit in wherever I needed to; to craft a mask that portrayed exactly what I believed others expected. As I became skilled at donning a variety masks, I buried my true self deeper and deeper within me. With every adaptation of myself to the culture around me, the mask grew tighter around my skin.

The next twenty years unleashed a progression of more adaptations. Ten years later (1996), I finally told a friend from church what had happened to me at the family reunion. She had disclosed her own experience of trauma during a group discussion and I recognized her as a safe person to open up with about my past. I was particularly relieved to discover I was not alone on this journey. Little did I know I was only taking my first of many steps on a long trail toward healing. There was a long, rigorous hike ahead and a lot of hard work left to be done. I really had no clue at that point what had been going on in my head and heart in the years that had passed. It wasn't until I was sitting in that counselor's office in 2006 and was confronted with the possibility that I was experiencing symptoms of PTSD that I began to allow the mess to unravel.

Another two years passed before I accepted that diagnosis and recognized that trauma-related stress isn't something that is "earned." Looking back, it sounds ridiculous. It's like I was saying I hadn't "earned the right" to be sick.

At one point I had a conversation with a retired Army Colonel about what I was facing. He offered an insight that abruptly shifted my perspective: "Veterans don't wear a diagnosis of PTSD as some sort of badge of honor. It's a wound that needs to heal like any other wound."

I needed to reset my concepts of trauma and stress. I had (and still have) a lot of learning to do.

As with any illness, diagnosing it is just one step in the process. Healing from it takes deliberate effort under the watchful, caring eyes of someone who knows how to navigate the complexities of what our brains are doing with the traumatic memories. I finally started that process in 2008, but it was another six years before I engaged in any effective therapy to work through the impact of trauma.

Through my recovery process, I learned to reframe the way I measure my own value. Instead of viewing my worth in terms of how well I had fit in or contributed to a specific community or social group, I accepted the truth that I had intrinsic value standing on my own.

Through my authenticity and vulnerability, I was contributing to the world around me in surprising ways. I began to see people for who they really are, not simply as a template that I needed to either avoid or emulate. I set out on a journey toward acceptance and authenticity: with myself and others. In the shadow of my freedom, my sense of personal value was taking on new levels of depth and meaning.

Chapter 4:
The Mask of Happiness

"It's a new day and I'm learning that the mind is at the same time our greatest asset and our greatest liability; it can help us to soar in the clouds or make us stumble in the dark."

It was New Year's Eve, 1997. For about two years I had lived in my church music director's basement. Most of that time I also served as his assistant on staff at the church. The relationship had not exactly soured, but it was not the great mentorship it had once been. I don't hold that against him. I've had many relationships with the church turn bitter; this wasn't one of them. I think in some ways we had just overstayed our welcome in each other's circles. It was time to move on. Unfortunately, I couldn't see it that succinctly at the time. All I saw was rejection.

There was a party going on upstairs. I sat on the small brick patio with the French doors to the living room wide open. I had laid the bricks to that patio and helped to hang those doors. In fact, he and I had taken a bare basement, framed the walls, added plumbing for a kitchen and bathroom, tiled the floors, and made a nice apartment out of it. As I listened to the hum of the guests' conversations and looked over our handiwork, thoughts of why things might be the way they were consumed me. Were the strangers upstairs mocking the hermit living in the basement? Were they replaying one of the many demo tapes I had given him in my more trusting days and having a nice chuckle at my expense? Did they pity me? Did they detest me? And would it be worse altogether if they simply had become unaware of my existence?

When thoughts betray us

It's not my earliest memory of distorted thinking and symptoms of social anxiety, but it is one of the clearest. In hindsight, I could very likely have walked up the stairs, "crashed" the party and been more than welcome. There were other events when I had had similar thought distortions only later to be asked why I had not come up for dinner or if I was feeling well. The greatest stigma that I faced existed in my own head and I was my own worst offender.

I often wonder, when it comes to issues I face in the mental health arena, what came first. Does depression feed social anxiety? Did the incongruency I felt in my gender presentation fuel my discomfort with socializing with men? Would it have been different if I had been allowed to socialize with women as a woman back then? Did my depression stem from the mental exhaustion of dealing with the complexity of all these topics? Were all of these merely byproducts of the latent, undiagnosed and untreated symptoms of post-traumatic stress?

Down and . . . I'm really too down for "out"

While I have some clear memories of warping and bending my interpretations of social interactions dating back to middle school, my experience with depression has been more subtle and subversive. After the assault in 1986, I started slipping in and out of depressive states. Doctors took stabs at other diagnoses such as Epstein-Barr virus and immune deficiencies. Not having any direct experience with any mental health issues in our family, we never really pursued the idea that this may be an illness above my neck and not below it. I like to think that had I been more forthcoming with information about the sexual assault, a more accurate diagnosis could have been reached. I'll never actually know. But this sense of always being on the brink of, or in the midst of a full-fledged depressive state dominates my memories of high school. Keep in mind: it was during these years that I was perfecting the art of the mask. People saw what I wanted, or thought I needed them to see, in order to maintain an illusion of having it all together.

Beginning to understand

In the spring of 2004, M and I were serving with a ministry as social directors for an apartment community. Once a month we stood at the gates with orange juice, coffee, and doughnuts or muffins and sent our residents off with well wishes for good days. On one particular day, sometime in the spring of 2004, I was feeling a bit distracted. I lacked the usual jovial engagement I aimed to bring to these events; my mask had some holes in it. Noticing my offbeat demeanor, M gently confronted me.

"You do remember what I told you last night, don't you?"

Of course I remembered. How could I not remember? She had taken a pregnancy test and it was positive. My response that morning had not changed much from the night before.

"We'll confirm it and cross that bridge when we need to."

Naturally, she was sure we were already standing squarely on that bridge and aptly saw my avoidance and delayed responses for what they were: unhindered fear.

I was attending school that spring, working toward finishing my bachelor's degree. I wasn't sure where we were headed post-graduation. She was working in a job she didn't like; I wasn't working at all. Our hands were full with the two kids we already had. A third child was not part of the equation. Not my equation anyway.

Looking back, I can't imagine my life without that news. Had I known then what I know now, I would still have been just as afraid — perhaps even more. But the child who was already taking shape as I mindlessly passed a muffin through another car window is now one of the greatest sources of joy in my life. In spite of her happy demeanor from very early in her life, we fought some deep, dark battles in our home those first few years.

A few weeks after an emergency C-section and complicated labor, M slipped into a severe bout of postpartum depression. Of course, I didn't see it that way at the time. The cycle of depressive episodes I had been battling for the last twenty years were only reinforced by her state of mind. I had finished my degree by that point and was working full time for the apartment ministry. The masks were fully intact and, in my own mind, they were more important than ever. People may not have been able to *see* the depression and anxiety that was dragging me under, but I can't imagine that they didn't *feel* it.

I perfectly understand that I have never been the "life of the party" type. The summer after I graduated from high school a longtime friend, and on-again, off-again crush, very plainly told me that

I was the type of person she could spend the rest of her life with, but for the time being she "just wanted to have fun." I was characterized as being funny and witty while at the same time having a depth that can make a person think, whether they wanted to or not. That persona enabled me to quite easily hide my depression. "Lost in a deep thought" is a look I pull off rather naturally. It becomes an easy mask for "I'm suffocating inside my own skin and I need help pulling myself through this."

August of 2007 brought my personal, emotional, and mental life to a head and ushered me toward the final failure of my carefully crafted masks. After serving with the apartment ministry since 2002 and being on staff since 2005, the president of the organization, my direct boss, informed me that my position was being eliminated. He gave me plenty of time to plan for the transition. Ultimately that meant more time for me to wander around the office overhearing muffled conversations that in all likelihood had nothing to do with me. My mind insisted otherwise. My anxiety and fear soared. The official story was that I was let go for financial reasons. I was working on some special projects and as money got tight for the organization, "special projects" became synonymous with "excess baggage." While for a long time I suspected there were more personal motives, I was eventually able to accept the reasons given. It was simply a tough time to be in any business related to the real estate market.

As I have gained a more nuanced understanding of what was happening in my mind during that season of life, I've wondered how much my depression and anxiety played a part in what happened with that job. I had visions for a long, deep future with this organization and the relationship seemed to come to an abrupt halt. When money gets tight in a small business or not-for-profit, salaries tend to fall into one of two categories: 1) operationally necessary to maintain either our mission, our cash flow or both and 2) none of the above. Had my depression put me into the "none of the above" category? If I had been more focused, had more clarity and vision, would I have found ways to be a more indispensable asset? Was it simply time for me to move on?

Depression held a pretty tight grip on me for the next seven years. Then the wheels, and the masks, all finally came off with a calamitous thunderclap stomping into my world.

The thought distortions still plague me. I frequently ask myself when I'm wrestling with a thought, "Is that the *most* true?" or "Is that something you can validate and if so does it really matter?" I am grateful for the way my mind works. I celebrate my ability to articulate a thought and thank God frequently for giving me opportunities to share that gift. I enjoy learning, reading and listening to new thoughts and weighing them against my core values and beliefs. But I have learned to acknowledge these gifts only after decades of experiencing the challenges of my own thought life. The line between productive thoughts and cognitive distortions is pencil thin, but powerful when I am able to work through it. Even still, I find myself wondering how long will this balance hold.

Chapter 5:
The Mask of Strength

"It's a new day and I'm learning that pain and suffering are personal, not relative. I can't compare mine to yours and you can't compare yours to mine. We can only love each other where we are."

The wrong story

As I've become more open and vulnerable with my story, I've had the privilege of hearing many others share their stories as well. Many of them are heartbreaking; many of them are incredibly inspirational. All of them are unique and all of them represent the path each individual's life has brought them down that makes them who they are today.

My life, like so many other lives, has had many twists and turns to it. At some point many of the stories that led me to where I am became unbelievable even to me. This became crystal clear a few years ago when I was at a Christmas party in my neighborhood. My parents also happened to be in town, something that doesn't happen as often as any of us would like. As the evening wore on, the conversation turned to stories of birth. Ours, our kids, our friends — they were all on the table.

When the time was right I offered the story of my own birth as I remembered it being told.

My dad was an active duty Naval officer at the time and was on sea duty. His ship, the USS Juneau, had been off the coast of Vietnam for most of Moms' pregnancy. It was 1972 and things were rather intense in that theater. As February and my due date approached, the ship was still a few days out to sea. Knowing that I could arrive at any moment, he worked his way into a ride on a mail helicopter. Just before they departed, he received word that Moms had gone into labor.

They were off the deck and heading for the California coastline as quickly as they could. Breaking protocol for this type of mission, the pilot radioed ahead and received permission to go straight to the rooftop of the hospital where I was to be born. They landed, and he made his way to the delivery ward within moments of my arrival.

As I finished the story I looked over at my parents and saw the look of amazement on their faces. At first I assumed they were simply impressed with my storytelling ability or with the detail with which I recounted the event. I was soon disappointed.

"That's a great story," Moms said breaking the silence. "It's nothing like it happened, but it's a great story!"

As it turns out, Dad had been at sea, but the ship arrived in port several days before I was born. They were scheduled to be out for a few days of exercises right afterward, but he was able to take leave and be home with us.

Needless to say I was rather crushed. This was boring. Not at all the adventurous, Indiana Jones-style kickoff to my life that I had conceptualized. It got even worse when I began to think about all the other stories and memories etched in my mind from my childhood. Had I distorted those as well? How did Dad find our first dog? What about the picnic on Sandia Peak outside of Albuquerque where I fell headfirst over the front seat of the car into a bucket of KFC chicken? What about the pinewood derby or soapbox derby competitions? Were they even real?

I spent the next few days going over some of my favorite stories with Moms and Dad and sorting out the distortions. None were as major as the story of my birth, but it provided a good walk down memory lane for all of us. When in a pinch at a party, the story of me messing up the story has been as productive as I had hoped the original story might be in terms of entertainment value.

Why we do that thing we do

Reeling from the shock of learning the epic story of my birth was less than accurate, I wondered why I had embellished and elaborated on the first moments of my life to the extent that my recollection barely resembled truth. I began to consciously observe others in my life, from preschoolers to pastors, engage in one-upmanship as they boasted about their successes and suffering. I embarked on a mental journey toward more authenticity and soon realized what people really need to hear was the truth. The things that *actually* happened are what truly resonated with people and evoked authentic, personal connection. A little obvious, perhaps, but I continue to be astonished at how many people feel the need to exaggerate their own experiences in an attempt to manage others' impressions of them. Apparently everyone wants to feel valued.

I am relieved that I don't have to be a good storyteller. I don't need to flaunt my creative versions of the truth or sprinkle in dramatic flair as I recount events of my life. I just need good memories and a heart of compassion to meet people where they are and share what is truly relevant to them; not simply for the sake of them knowing me better, but also to help them know themselves better. Honestly sharing our hurts and burdens invites others into a personal, sacred space. From there we can get down to the real business of life: healing hurts and growing more beautiful from the inside out. When we do it well, we invite them to do the same. We all win.

There are many stories in my life that fit the bill of being "share worthy" in the right moment. Many of them are printed in these pages, many more are on my blog and still many others will have to wait for future projects and personal conversations. Perhaps one of the most powerful and life changing was when I took on one of my greatest adversaries: me.

An early version of this appeared in a blog post from March 2015 called "Marching On."

Marching on

It was a cloudy day in March 2014 that I decided would be the last day of my life.

There were several things that led to that decision. I worked for a mortgage company where my job was to either keep people out of foreclosure or try to win the legal battles necessary to foreclose. Having just lost our home the year before, the job often served as an emotional trigger.

The weekend before this, my wife had asked me for a divorce. She had done this before, or simply given me her rings, but this time she also insisted I leave the house. She had just discovered emails I had exchanged with a friend discussing the possibility that I was in an emotionally abusive marriage. There were also emails to one of my female physical therapists that she thought were too personal in nature. She may have been right. I was emotionally lost in the marriage and very likely would have been drawn to anyone who showed a degree of compassion and understanding, even if it was on a professional level. The emails were addressing professional issues, but with a personal flair. Regardless, I spent that Friday night in a hotel. We reconciled the next morning but tensions were mounting.

I was also facing mounting frustrations in my medical care. In 1989 I was first hospitalized for abdominal pain. The symptoms had persisted with multiple hospitalizations, ER visits, scans and an appendectomy — all with no relief and no diagnosis. On that March morning in 2014 I had a follow-up appointment with a surgeon to review a recent MRI. The diagnosis: psychosomatic. The pain, according to him, was in my head.

I had had enough. Instead of going to work after the appointment, I stopped at a local sporting goods store. I knew I could buy a gun and be done with it. I had guns at home but they were all family heirlooms; I couldn't taint them with what had to be done. As I was getting ready to sign the papers and have the background check done for the purchase, I hesitated. What stopped me was a simple thought, "How am I going to explain to my wife that I spent this money on a gun?"

The thought made me aware of a very important fact: somewhere in my mind I planned on having to give an account for the money. *I planned to be alive.*

That realization triggered other thoughts about my kids, my parents, and our church. I remembered a contract I had signed with a therapist after a past brush with suicidal ideation. The contract was simply a plan to prevent me from following through with exactly what I was now determined to do. I told the clerk at the gun counter that I was having second thoughts about the purchase and needed to think it over.

Returning to my truck I fought through the tears that were streaming down my face and started making calls. By the end of the day I had voluntarily admitted myself to a hospital where I knew I would be safe — safe from my past, safe from my thoughts, and, for the moment, safe from myself.

I spent a little over a week in the hospital and began an intensive outpatient program soon after my release. We focused on various techniques and exercises based in cognitive behavioral therapy and I began to engage in the process of rethinking just about everything. As I look back on all that transpired the following year, I am both grateful for and humbled by the life I am privileged to live. I still battle with depression and anxiety, I still have major stress triggers in my life, but I have come to accept three things about the nature of change that helps me press on. (If you're familiar with the Serenity Prayer, you will quickly recognize the similar themes.)

First, everything will change. There is nothing that is immune to that reality except God, and even then our understanding of God is constantly evolving. When I think of all the things that scare me about my episodes of severe depression, what scares me the most is the *myth of permanence* — believing that everything will always be exactly as I perceive it to be at the moment. The reality behind the myth is that when things feel most dark, they will change. The darkness will not last forever.

Second, I have a greater ability to change than I give myself credit for. I have vastly sold myself short in my ability to take hold of my health, my emotions, my identity, and several other key areas of life. For a number of reasons, most of them based on very strong thought distortions, I had surrendered those things to the influences of others. Becoming "me" meant taking back the control I had needlessly yielded.

Finally, the things I can't control or change don't matter nearly as much as they feel like they do in a moment of desperation. One of the best lessons I have learned this year is to maintain a healthy perspective on those parts of my life over which I have no control. The opinions of others, medical developments, job-related issues — they are all going to happen with or without my consent and worry. While they may be unpleasant, uncomfortable, or stressful, I don't have to allow them into the core of who I am.

One of the most significant breakthroughs in the months after I left the hospital was that the chronic pain I had been dealing with was finally diagnosed. I had been working with an endocrinologist for several years trying to correct extremely low testosterone levels. It was counterintuitive for me, but as a married man, I was hoping it might also help "cure" my identity issues as well. Regardless, the hormones just made me more sick and emotionally unstable. We had also been monitoring a testicular cyst. With the failure of the hormone therapy, I returned to a urologist for a follow-up. We discovered the cyst had more than doubled in size over the course of a year. I made the decision to have it, along with the testicle, removed. During the procedure, it was discovered that blood flow to the remaining testicle had been cut off. It was essentially dead as well. Furthermore, the urologist performing the procedure, observed herniation in the abdominal wall — fat and nerve tissue protruding through the muscles that make up the base of my core muscles.

After several more scans, a general surgeon agreed to repair bilateral inguinal hernias. He went in prepared to patch the small space at the opening of the inguinal canal with a piece of mesh about the size of a half dollar on each side. After cleaning up the area, he discovered not two, but seven points of herniation. When all was said and done, there were two 5 square inch mesh pieces sewn into my abdominal wall.

After 25 years of beating my head against a wall I was finally free of the pain. The surgeries that corrected the issues also helped to identify and correct the hormone imbalances that had been baffling doctors. I began a regimen to bring my estrogen levels to a therapeutic level. In less than three months, I went from eight prescription medications for everything from anxiety to insomnia, down to two. I still take an antidepressant and a low dose of hormones. There are still challenges and struggles ahead, but I know I am on the right path.

I experienced God's grace and compassion that year. I am thankful to not only be alive, but to be engaging in life. I look forward to more great years and more awesome changes to come.

Reclaiming March

I don't know what may be trying to kill you or someone you know, if anything. You may not know exactly. You may be struggling with depression and anxiety and a life of past hurts that make my story look like a cakewalk. You may be struggling and reading my stories and thinking, "I've never been through that — I don't deserve to suffer."

Stop it. Now. Your pain, your suffering, is as personal to you as mine is to me. It matters because it is that pain that has shaped you and will continue to shape you until you intentionally begin the journey out of it. There is no need to exaggerate or embellish your story to make it feel more worthy of the hurt it has brought to your life. Your story is personal to you, not relative to me, and it makes you unique in this big, mad, crazy world.

On March 26, 2016, two years to the day after I wrestled with my own will to live, I made another choice. I had been baptized as an infant, and again in college to appease my fundamental classmates who turned up their noses on my infant baptism. Finally understanding that God desires a beautiful life for me, full of grace and love despite its many complexities, I chose to be baptized into a new stage of life. This time it was my choice. For my own reasons. For my own affirmation of life.

Chapter 6:
The Mask of Control

"It's a new day and I'm learning that it takes as much courage to accept what we cannot change as it does to change what we can."

Whether it's shifting the way I relate to people, my gender expression, or my faith expression, the last couple of years of my life have been marked by change. Like most people, change can spark deep fear in me. Courage has been described both as calmness in the face of fear and as what is left when fear, trembling, and running are no longer an option. I will never get tired of saying or quoting the serenity prayer; in fact that prayer is the inspiration for this "new day" quote. The prayer reminds me that through peace or serenity, we will be equipped to accept what we cannot change. Likewise, through courage we will be able to change the things that need to be changed.

I've also found great comfort in reversing those concepts. Not just because I'm in a frame of mind in which I question everything, but because my life experience proves it out: it takes great peace to endure great change and it takes great courage to accept and step away from things we cannot change. Needing wisdom to know the difference between them is a constant. I'm just not willing to mess around with certain pieces of my life.

Accepting and changing

March of 2014 ushered in an intense season of evaluation and discernment. It was a time of sorting all of life into one of two categories: change or accept. It was also a time when I was gathering courage and actively seeking serenity, knowing full well that whatever was coming down the pike, I was going to need an abundance of both.

Some people and things that made it into the category of acceptance, knowing I could never change them:

- My wife – Her heart and mind are her territory and there was little I could, or should do to try and affect change in them.

- My kids – Except to watch them grow and lovingly nurture them along the way, I wouldn't even want to change them.

- My past – The hurts and highs are what they are. There is nothing to be done about them except to better manage the memories.

- God – God isn't changing. My understanding of God, my perception of God, and my experience of God are all in flux, but the character and essence of who God is won't change. In other words, I don't see God as a moving target.

- My self-perception – this is somewhat counter to the goal of most of the therapy I've ever been in. We are often told to aim at restoring distorted thoughts and ground them in reality; we strive to turn negative images and experiences into positive energy and direction. But what I came to accept in this season was that the core of my identity — the way I perceive "me" and on which all other concepts of self are built — was woven into the essence of my being long ago. Among those central beliefs was the awareness that my gender is feminine and that I identify culturally as a woman.

With the process of acceptance underway, I turned my focus to change.

Change is never simple. That's why I contend that it requires ample amounts of courage *and* serenity. Change that involves tearing down the very basics of your belief system, family structure, persona, and public image is remarkably intense. Suffice it to say, I don't really think I knew what I was getting myself into. I just knew I had no choice but to go there. So I did.

- I moved out of the house. The act of stepping out of a house that held a large stable of painful memories was an essential first step in clearing the way for all that was to come. Eventually I moved onto a houseboat. That environment provided the background and inspiration for the way my life took shape in the months to come. It also provided an atmosphere of peace and tranquility that I would need as a refuge to reflect on my life: past, present, and future.

- I started building new social networks. Up to that point, my social life had been deeply entwined in my wife's and vice versa. We were focused on either our church or our community, which was mostly the neighborhood where we lived or the schools the kids attended. My new social networks were driven by my interests and desires; people I wanted to get to know and spend time with regardless of age, gender, or life-stage.

- I found a new church. This was a particularly difficult task. The church plant we had been involved with had disbanded and the leadership was clear that they did not approve of the direction my life was going. The church and I had been one too many rounds, and I was quite ready to be done with it. I wasn't ready to be done with God. I wasn't ready to be done with people. I knew that if I wanted to experience the best of both, I would have to re-engage with the church in some form. It took some time, but I landed among a ragamuffin group of sojourners who, like me, were just grateful for each day we were gifted with another breath.

My expectations of God, the church, and each other were incredibly low. Surprisingly, with that as the standard, my sense of connection, acceptance, and community has not only met those low expectations, but has soared above all previous notions of what church should be. When I first started attending Serenity Church, I made the statement that I had been to all the other churches on the block; this was the last one left that would have me. My fellow "Serenitarians" confirmed the same experience.

While I may have landed at Serenity Church out of desperation, it is my love for those people and my understanding of the clear work God is doing in our hearts and lives that keeps me there. My experience over the last year has proven that I have many choices of churches that would accept me with open arms, but I have found a home.

- I took control of my medical care. Medical issues had been lingering for years with little to no progress. The tension and despair of undiagnosed pain had taken its toll on me physically, emotionally, mentally, and spiritually. I found some new doctors and a new therapist and we pressed forward.

- I took off the masks. The mask that said I had it all together. The mask that said I was the "man" this world said I should be. The mask that said I had no pain or struggles. They didn't just fall off, they cracked and shattered. From behind them emerged a somewhat shy, but eerily confident woman that much resembled the person I had always seen myself to be. I had a great deal of growing up to do.

Many people who go through this gender transition refer to it as a second puberty. For me it felt like I was finally completing the first one; a coming of age over 20 years in the making. I breathed deeply, sighed heavily, and started to figure out how I fit into my new world as myself, as a woman. The challenge would be to allow myself to fit into the world, not to simply create new masks to make myself fit.

The excitement, energy, and, yes perhaps even desperation, gave me the courage to move forward despite the blaring questions that shouted with whispers in my head: Could I live with a new level of honesty with others and myself? Was it possible for me to establish and hold healthy boundaries? Would I learn to recognize the old masks and be able to admit it if I started trying to piece them back together? Could I find people I could trust to reflect those moments in my life back to me?

The biggest change in the last year has been my gender presentation. Just for emphasis, I will say it again: the *biggest* change in the last year has been my gender presentation.

Expressing my gender openly has precipitated so many other changes in friendships, doctrine, and perspectives on social justice. There have been a few moments and principles that really speak to the power of change in our lives.

A rose is a rose

Names mean something to me. They carry not only an association with a particular physical person, but also with the particular personality. I know as I have talked with others and read about the experience of other transgender people it has been made clear that there are as many ways to land on a name as there are transgender people. Mine has some meaning behind it. I stayed up nearly all night one weekend reading and wrestling until I landed on something that fit my self-perception and would be a constant reminder to me of my journey. That one night of contemplation capitalized on a lifetime of desiring to be set free. I captured what my new feminized name means to me in a blog post:

"Laura" is a name I've always known worked for me. I think it may go back to my affinity for Laura Ashley when I was younger. It comes from the word "laurel," the plant used by Greeks and Romans for making wreaths to crown the heads of victors in sport and battle. I wanted a name to go with it that symbolized my new chance at a healthy life. Bethany is the town in the New Testament where Jesus raised Lazarus from the dead. Together, they stand for a victorious new life! (posted on Jan. 24, 2015, sophiasojourn.com)

One defining moment of change was the first time I introduced myself as "Laura Beth" to a group of people. The group was a divorce support group that had become the core of my new social life. I had prepared myself for a reaction. There was going to be a gasp and shock at what I was sharing and asking people to do. It was one of many times that I geared up for a conflict only to be met instead with understanding and acceptance. It is the group's practice to introduce ourselves as we went around the circle and shared about how we were doing. When my turn came, I shared that I was moving forward not only in my divorce, but also in my own understanding of myself. To help with that, I asked them to start calling me by my new name, Laura Beth. There were nods and acknowledgements and the meeting went on as usual. The lack of "gasp" and "shock" was pleasantly disappointing.

To whom much is given

The example of acceptance and grace that I was given over my name that night prompted me to think carefully about what I expected from others. Acceptance of transgender people has come a long way in recent years. There are still many questions that well-intentioned people have about how to respond to us. One simple area of confusion is in how to talk to and about us. Again, there are as many different thoughts on the use of names and gender pronouns as there are transgender people, but I decided that grace for others should be the principal that drives me.

For those who have known me a long time, adjusting to my new name is challenging. I'll give them grace.

For the cashier or stranger in the grocery store that "mis-genders" me (uses "he" instead of "she," etc.), I understand that they are on their own journey and I don't really know how I fit into it at that particular moment. I will give them grace.

For those on a journey of wrestling with how my gender identity intersects with their understanding of God and the God created the gender of humanity, I have been there and still carry the scars of those mental, academic and emotional battles. I will give them grace.

The rule of the day is grace. It's what I hope to receive and I am pleased to be able to give it.

The transition period for a transgender person is incredibly personal. It will never look the same for two people, regardless of how much effort the mental and medical health communities put into standardizing the process. Since my journey has primarily been about taking off masks, I have been reluctant to put on a new mask in the name of gender identity. My voice is my voice (and has always been toned toward the feminine side). I wear things that make me comfortable: sometimes jeans and a T-shirt, sometimes a skirt and a blouse. When it comes to others' responses to me, regardless of their intentions, I remind myself that they are entitled to their own journey. It then becomes a privilege to potentially be a catalyst toward more open and gracious understanding lives and people on those journeys.

The cornerstone of my identity

I sometimes forget what a privilege hindsight is. The ability to peer into the past, know a little more about all the puzzle pieces, and smugly judge my younger self for not being able to put it all together is priceless. It's not unlike watching the protagonist of dramatic film fumble through the plot, not knowing what we as the audience know about how their enemies are scheming against them. We watch her walk right into a carefully laid trap, holding our breath in hopes that she picks up on the clues in time to avoid disaster.

I tend to replay moments of my life in the same way. If I had known this, heard that, or seen the other, I would have responded differently in any given situation. There always seems to be a single pivot point in the plot that brings the whole thing together; a corner piece that, once it is set in place, brings order to the whole mess.

I found my corner piece in the process of deconstructing everything I held as true. My faith. My doctrine. My relationships. All of them were stripped back to one simple truth that I refused to release: God is either sovereign or not. I choose to believe that God is sovereign.

Order in the chaos

With that view of God as my anchor, I began to re-examine myself, Scripture, and the world around me. I'm still working through the reconstruction process, but in the midst of it I am engaging in new perceptions of the intersection of my faith and gender identity.

Sipping yet another cup of coffee and clamoring away on my keyboard, trying to articulate the emergence of my transgender identity, I feel frustrated with the difficulty in expressing how I came to terms with it. At some point, a rather humbling thought occurred to me: *Have I come to terms with it?* After nearly six years of counseling, a lifetime of wrestling, and more than a year in transition, I still have only begun to comprehend what it really means to be transgender.

The first thing I remembered admitting to myself about my gender identity was "I am not a man." Looking back, this insight unlocked a new lens through which I have come to understand myself. The way I relate to people, the way I approach work and parenting, and the way I process emotions are all much more aligned with what we culturally view as feminine. That's not to say I didn't have my "man" moments; in fact I still have them. I fix my own cars (although if I could afford to pay someone else to do it, I would). I'm teaching my kids about fishing and boating: all things that we might culturally describe as "masculine." It's not that girls can't or shouldn't do them, it's just not typically how our social construct works.

It was another few years before I was comfortable thinking of myself as a woman. I first had to go through the process of deconstructing my masculine concept of self as it had been ingrained in me. This is what shattering the masks is all about. I was, for the first time in my life, exploring who I was, not who I was trained and benevolently conditioned by society to be.

Living in a state of transition is one of the greatest challenges to my identity that I have faced to date. I'm taking the inner turmoil and displaying it for the world to see. My confusion becomes the confusion of every family member, coworker, fellow student, church member, professor, close friend, and total stranger. From my own parents to the store cashier, questions as simple as "he" or "she," "ma'am" or "sir" suddenly take on a whole new depth. As I noted earlier, my attitude has been to have grace for the confusion of others, but in doing so I have downplayed my own confusion. While I solidly identify as "she" and "ma'am," patience for this process is what having grace for myself looks like, while I continue to strive toward having grace for others.

Change is a challenge, and whether we are dealing with the "accept what we can't" or "do what we can" columns, courage and serenity are the order of the day. The only thing I know with any certainty is that something else is about to change. What will it be? When will it be? (That's why books have sequels.)

Chapter 7:

The Mask of Emotions

"It's a new day and I'm learning that if my mind is to truly find its voice, my heart must also find its song."

The "feeling" void

For about a year after my brush with suicidal plans, I worked through the process of unmasking myself and finding some sense of my true identity. While I was in the hospital, a care provider told me that I was "unable to connect with my emotions." As I wrestled to unwind and redirect various thought patterns, I continued under that assumption. I believe her intention was good; in truth, I *wasn't* connecting with my emotions. Whenever the need to process an event or concept arose, I went straight in for the analytical kill. I had answers. I had thoughts. Good ones. They had carried me this far and they were good enough to carry me further.

Then again, I was lying there on a lumpy hospital bed after an episode of suicidal ideation that had progressed into an actual plan. I was suffocating in a rapidly deteriorating marriage and I was incredibly confused about my own identity. How effective were my thoughts, really? How reliable were the concepts that constantly required me to find just the right personality disguise for any given moment? Perhaps it was time to give this whole idea of *feeling* a chance.

Reconnecting

A therapist told me that I needed to work on expanding my emotional vocabulary, so I dove into the deep end and gave it my all. Confident in this highfalutin method of identifying and expressing emotions, she handed me graphs to compare levels of emotional connection, charts that showed how emotions interact with each other, and wheels that provided more specific words to describe my emotions. I meticulously assigned colors to the different emotions varying in shades of intensity. If there was a logical way to process emotions, I was determined find it and make it work, every time, all the time. Somewhere along that path, reality kicked in. That approach to experiencing "my feels" quickly proved to be futile. If I was going to get a grip on this whole emotional side of me, I was just going to have to let go and start to *feel*.

After my separation from M, I needed a place to live. Finding an apartment I could afford somewhere close to the kids where I would be comfortable with them proved to be a challenge. I toyed with the idea of living in a fifth wheel trailer. While looking at options on Craigslist, I came across a houseboat for rent. That particular vessel was less than desirable, but I was hooked on the idea. I found an old houseboat that needed a great deal of TLC, but was solid and had plenty of space. The boat was nameless so I christened her "Sophia Sojourn," my journey to wisdom.

Sophia sat in a slip on a decent-sized lake with her bow pointed eastward. The open space on the bow became my morning sanctuary. I saw and heard the lake's wildlife come to life as the spinning earth turned to once again allow the sun's rays to fall on my face. Taking deep, deliberate breaths, I worked through this mantra, clearing my mind and setting aside the anxiety that sought to take up residence in my soul.

Breathing in, "Soli deo gloria" . . . giving God the center place in my life, even as my concept of God is ever expanding.

Breathing out, "Soli Christo" . . . acknowledging the role Christ plays in my healing, even as my understanding of that role is being reshaped.

Breathing in, "Pneumas, Ruach" . . . the Greek and Hebrew words for the Spirit of God, invoking the presence of the Holy Spirit as I look for peace and growth.

Breathing out, "7, 6, 5, 4, 3, 2, 1" . . . working to simply focus on the life-giving breath that is feeding both my body and spirit.

Time and time again, I breathed these calming thoughts, sometimes in my head, sometimes out loud. Once I gained a sense of clarity, I allowed the thoughts from the previous day space in my consciousness. I tended to the images brought up in dreams as I slept, and if any of them caused anxiety, I would return to my breathing prayer as a grounding place. It was during these morning sessions that I first started journaling my thoughts about the lessons each new day held. On one particular morning, something clicked. I felt something. I actually *felt* something.

The lake was on fire with the days emerging light. The herons and ducks were stretching their wings and venturing out of their nesting spots. I don't know if it was the warmth of the sun or the gentle breeze rocking the boat, but I was transported back to a more innocent time when I experienced emotions with more freedom, with more abandon and with fewer walls guarding my heart and soul. I found myself back on the beaches of Puerto Rico, right near the cliffs that separated our neighborhood from the blue water crashing into the shore beneath them.

I remembered sitting there and composing poems and songs, deep from the heart — at least as deep as a twelve-year-old heart can reach — and being free of concerns driven by concepts such as logic, practicality, and responsibility. I remembered specific verses, even though the papers that held them have long since been lost:

> *The sun is setting on the deep blue sea;*
> *As I sail in its reflection, this is the song it sings:*
> *'Home is where you are going;*
> *Home from the sea;*
> *Home is where you are going;*
> *Where you ought to be.'*

There were dozens of them and they reflected what I felt as clearly as the water reflected the sunrise. Flooded with these memories, hope and courage washed over me. Somewhere in my soul, a desire for adventure was reborn. The contrast of those innocent memories with my emotionally stifled present reality jolted my mind back to the comment of that caretaker from the hospital. Was I actually *unable* to emote, or had I truly come to *fear* my emotions?

Beyond the fear of feeling

Strong emotions are a source of energy for me. Over the years, as I confronted the stress and anxiety emanating from my marriage, my career, and the failing masks of my self-identity, the energy of the emotions became overwhelming. I never developed the skills I needed to contain and channel that energy into something valuable and productive. It became the pariah of my soul. The value of the mind soon outweighed the value of the heart. First I lost my song, then I lost my voice — those unique qualities that set each of us apart from the rest of God's creation — and eventually I lost myself.

Something changed as I sat cross-legged on Sophia's bow, quieting my mind and opening my heart to new thoughts and ideas. The memories of the moments that came from engaging the emotions of my youth blended with the wisdom that comes with years.

They weren't overwhelming.

They were filling.

They weren't frightening.

They were motivating.

They didn't make me want to crawl in a hole.

They made me want to sing from a rooftop.

The emotions I permitted to creep into my awareness were not all pleasant, but they were powerful; and so was the energy that I found in them. It wasn't long before I realized I could use that energy to connect with people. It was that energy that I channeled into my writing. It wasn't controlling my emotions that proved to be the key to finding more peace in my life; it was the willingness to embrace them in their raw, unedited, uncensored form.

Unlike those evenings on the cliffs of the Caribbean, I don't have the luxury of dreamy moments void of the shackles of responsibility. I wouldn't even want such a thing. The same things that provide joy in my life — my kids, my boat, my friendships, and more — all come with commitments and responsibilities. There is a balance to be found to be sure. But unlocking the song of my heart has opened the door to experiencing life with a new zeal and confidence.

Shattering Masks

Chapter 8:
The Mask of Pain

"It's a new day and I'm learning that we can't un-see what we have seen, we can't un-feel what we have felt and we can't put back on masks that have been shattered."

I love Westerns. One of my favorite plot lines is the story of the sidekick, the secondary hero. They are on the sidelines, mild mannered and of few words. What they do have to say is incredibly relevant, often keeping the protagonist focused and on the right track. Women just as easily fill the role as men, though the genre as a whole still has some severe stereotype issues to overcome.

Almost without fail, just before the white hats and the black hats have their final showdown at high noon, the supporting character is finally pushed over the brink. He can only take so much. He can only watch until this one person, child, horse, or dog is put in harm's way. Then he snaps; and he snaps big. If there is a gang of ten outlaws and our hero is riding to a showdown with the gang leader, the mild-mannered sidekick with his pent-up rage, now unbridled, will take out the other nine in an unexpected show of force and skill. He finally has his say. He finally pulls the trigger.

Adjusting the hairpins

When working with a firearm, a "hairpin trigger" is designed so that there is as little pull length in the motion of the trigger as possible. Unsafe, they are not for the novice shooter to manage. It's the hairpin trigger that will likely cause the quick-draw competitor to limp to the hospital with a bullet in the toe of her boot.

Knowing my emotional triggers is one of the keys to managing my mental health. For decades it felt like when any of my negative emotions or memories were triggered, I responded like a dutiful soldier defending a hilltop. Like a hairpin trigger on an automatic rifle, I would open up and lay down as many rounds of ammunition as I could until I felt "safe." My rapid fire produced more innocent casualties than any actual defense from real harm.

My new M.O. is to respond more like a musketeer. When the trigger happens, I pull out my powder and a musket ball. I load the barrel with powder, drop the ball, and pack it with the ramming rod — being sure to pull the ramming rod out of the barrel (it's not a good thing to shoot a three-foot-long iron rod down range). I prime the pan with powder, lock the hammer, and finally pull the stock to my shoulder.

By this time I have had a second to breathe. The intensity of whatever triggered me has had a moment to subside and I stop and ask myself if I really need to "pull the trigger," and if so, what that action might need to look like. More than likely it will have more to do with a well-coordinated retreat and engaging with grace and compassion than mounting a full frontal assault.

And on a side note: professional musketeers used to accomplish reloading in seconds. For me it takes a whole lot longer with an excellent chance of an eventual misfire.

Here is a real-life example from a couple of years ago.

What happened

I wouldn't wish repeating middle and early high school years on my greatest enemy. I've already shared about the darkness of those years in my life, but I am well aware that even without the extra burden of trauma, they are tough years to weather emotionally and physically. Perhaps the only thing worse than going through them ourselves is having to watch our kids go through them and only be able to speak into the process from a loving, albeit protective, distance.

A few years ago, when my son was in sixth grade, he began to self-harm as an emotional outlet. We had experienced this with his older sister as well. When he confided in her about his problem, she wisely broke his confidence and shared the news with M. We worked with him as best we could by providing access to a counselor, opening communication lines, and being as attentive as we could for future warning signs. Self-harm is an addiction. Like all addictions, it doesn't begin overnight and it doesn't go away overnight either.

It had been a few months since I first learned of his self-injuring. I was sitting in our home office one evening and M brought our son in to see me. They had paper towels held onto spots on his arms and she, admirably, remained rather calm. There were streams of blood dripping down his arms toward his hands from the thin gashes of a razor. The bright red streaks took me back to a morning nearly thirty years earlier.

What my mind saw

It was a Sunday morning in 1979. The details, like most traumatic experiences, are in some places really fuzzy and in others as clear as a bell.

"Bus is leaving in five minutes," Dad hollered from the bottom of the stairs. It was the prompt we needed to find the last missing shoe, finish brushing teeth or tuck in a shirttail so that Moms wouldn't do it in public as we walked across the parking lot into church.

We climbed into our maroon Caprice Classic and headed to a prayer breakfast at Oaklette United Methodist Church in Chesapeake, Virginia. I loved prayer breakfasts. Not for the prayer, that came much later in life. I loved eating pancakes while sitting at the long tables in the fellowship hall. I loved the ice-cold milk out of a Styrofoam cup. I loved the hum and chatter of adult conversation that was way over my head, figuratively and literally. None of that was to be this particular morning.

We drove through an intersection, passing underneath a green traffic light, and I saw a car coming toward us with no hint of slowing down. In my memory it was green and it came at us in an arch, as if it was somehow following the curve of the earth. I was later told the car was blue. I don't know why it matters, but it will always be green in my mind. I was sitting in the back, left seat. Kayla was to my right, dad was driving, and Moms was in the front passenger seat.

The car struck us with the deafening sound of metal colliding with metal and each side giving way to the intensity of the impact. We spun toward the curb at the corner of the busy intersection. The impact knocked me over and I found myself laying on my side on the seat of the car. Confused, it took a few moments for me to realize it was me who was on my side and not the car. From that angle, I had a clear view as my sister was catapulted over the front and her head cracked the windshield. The spinning car brought her back over the seat where she struck her head on the dome light before landing back in the seat next to me. She was conscious, but couldn't get a deep enough breath to even cry.

I found my voice as I looked at Kayla and as dad turned around to see if we were okay. Both of their faces were covered by streams of the blood that poured out of their foreheads, faces, and mouths. I couldn't move. I was paralyzed with fear and although uncut, had broken my collarbone and dislocated a hip. Being 1979 and long before any laws were in place to mandate them, Moms was the only one wearing a seatbelt that day. She eventually stepped out of the crippled car with a big bruise on her arm.

Ambulances, police cars, and news crews soon flooded the scene. Dad had pulled blankets from the trunk and laid them on the sidewalk before pulling the two of us from the back seat. He and Kayla were the first to be loaded onto stretchers and rushed to the hospital. Paramedics had immobilized my legs, but sat me in a seat toward the front of the ambulance. Moms sat close as the crew loaded a stretcher with an older woman in a neck brace. I would learn later that she had been driving the green (blue) car. As we pulled away and the sirens blared to life, Moms found the courage to ask a paramedic if everyone was going to be okay. He informed her that there was a little girl who he didn't think was going to survive. Moms immediately began praying for who she assumed was a little girl in the other car. As it turned out, there was only one young girl in the accident that day.

I don't remember anything of what happened at the hospital, only that a family friend had come to take me home while Moms and Dad stayed behind with Kayla. With the television on to keep me distracted from the fear and pain, a news report came on with coverage of the accident. The reporter announced that my sister had died from her injuries. Frantically rushing to change the channel or turn off the television, the family friend who was taking care of me tried to reassure me that everything was going to be okay and that the reporter had made a mistake. But I had heard it with my own ears - on the television. It had to be true. My sister was gone, I was sure of it.

This was long before the days when a cell phone could provide instant access to a parent who could have reassured me that all was well. It seemed like hours before I heard one of their voices on the phone. Dad and Kayla each had hundreds of stitches in their heads, but neither of their injuries proved to be life-threatening. I went to visit her in the hospital nearly a week later and was not prepared to see her stitched and bandaged. It was many years later that I finally opened up to her about the guilt I felt from not being able to look at her that day. I just stared out of her hospital window with panic taking a tight grip on my heart.

My collarbone soon healed; my hip had healed much quicker. The car was replaced; surgeries masked the scars left on the skin. I had blissfully assumed that once bones mend and blood stops flowing, the incident was over and done with. It wasn't until I began to explore the ramifications of PTSD that I started to connect the dots between specific nightmares and occasional panic attacks on the road that I fully acknowledged the impact of the events that day.

Back to here and now

As I sat in the office inspecting my son's arms, images from the car accident flashed through my mind and I began to "load the musket." Before I could even pull out the powder cask, I had switched gears and was assessing the wounds. Protective parenting spoke more loudly than past fear. We drove to the ER and faced the barrage of questions about how we were going to help keep him safe. The staff was kind and compassionate — to both of us.

Once I knew he was safe and cared for, I needed to let the memories that were triggered by his incisions have their moment in the light. Eventually I saw both moments — in the Virginia intersection and my home office in Texas — as a mask being ripped from my face. I learned that once it came off, there was no putting it back on. Sometimes, like the mask of innocence, I wished I could put it back on. It had come off too soon, in my opinion. Recently however, as living without the masks has led to more integrity and authenticity, the temptation to put them back on is easier and easier to resist.

To my knowledge that was the last of his self-harm incidents. It was a wake-up call. Not that life got all cheery and hummingbirds started following him around as he whistled through the halls of the school, but he did the hard work to find new ways of coping with his emotional pain in a healthy way.

As for me, I accepted that I can't "un-feel" my feelings, I can't "un-see" what I have seen, and, Lord willing, I can't hide behind masks once they have been shattered.

Shattering Masks

Chapter 9:

The Mask of Affection

"It's a new day and I'm learning that there is as much if not more value in being wanted or desired in a relationship than there is in being needed."

My thoughts and my emotions began to find a stronger balance. They were more even and productive. Feelings became more real, thoughts became truer, and life started to make more sense — not complete sense, but more sense. For example, my perspective on relationships changed. In the months after my divorce had been finalized, I had serious doubts about my ability to be in a romantic relationship. I wasn't even sure I wanted to be in one.

The new balance of thought and emotion I was finding helped me see the idea of companionship through a healthier lens. I could finally say with certainty that I truly believe I was designed for companionship. In fact, I think, with rare exceptions, we were all designed that way. The person who can function at her peak without someone in her life who knows her every strength and weakness and loves her anyway, is rare; it's a gift that she has been given. To take on a project or a cause without the entanglements of another life has its marked advantages. But for most of us, the cost that comes with giving up intimacy, from losing the energy and sense of security we find in friendships, is high. The joy, pleasure, peace, and intensity we feel in romantic relationships are not elements of life we are quick to sacrifice; nor should anyone ever have to make that sacrifice.

A new perspective

As I stepped into this journey of self-discovery, the whole paradigm of relationships has taken on a new level of meaning in my life. Just like the reconstruction of my faith, I am challenging my idea of what relationships are "supposed" to look like. It's not something I believe can happen overnight, or even in a month or two. It's not something that can happen isolated in a think tank or in my own mind. It's something that requires me to get emotionally messy, to head out to the front lines of life and engage people on a more vulnerable level. I fully expect genuine pain and intense joy as I work through the process.

There have been several steps to paving the way for this to happen, and frankly I'm still working through them. For one thing, I have had to explore the pieces and parts of me that have made relating to people challenging for the bulk of my life. Whether I label it as codependency or chalk it up to a deeply rooted identity crisis, I have brought toxic elements to more friendships and intimate relationships than I really care to admit. I am still sorting it all out; I'm certain it will be a lifelong process. The core of this evolution has been the practice of creating healthy personal boundaries. Maintaining those boundaries has also revealed a tendency to jump from passive people pleasing straight to aggressive self-defense. The new goal, which I am achieving with moderate success, is regulated and loving assertiveness.

Another basic element of my future romantic encounters is becoming comfortable with the idea of identifying as a woman who is attracted to women. I never thought I would identify as a lesbian. As I have taken a fearless inventory of my heart *and* mind on the subject, the idea of a label that defines my future relationships feels much like jumping into one of the very boxes that I just spent a great deal of time and energy breaking out of. My aim is to live life to its fullest and in the process of that find someone who is doing the same and consequently headed down the same paths that I am walking. Dating is not a priority, although I desire the companionship of a woman who shares my passions and joys in life. *Living* is my objective and I have faith that true companionship will come from that endeavor.

That writes well as a theory, but I have to admit the reality still perplexes me. Questions that I once took for granted have been haunting my mind. *Who would be attracted to me? Why? What does the relationship look like? With the physical changes that have occurred, what does sex look like? With the changes that have taken place in my view of God, do I still believe the same things about sex that I always have?* When I allow myself to be a discoverer on the journey and not an orchestrator of the details, my raging codependency starts to surface. In my efforts to please everyone, I try and think ahead of all the people around me. More than that, I usually start to think *for* other people. Not only is that rather exhausting, but it also robs me of experiencing the diversity of thought and perspective that is naturally built into all of our social networks. By projecting myself into people's thoughts, I lose out on truly getting to know *them.* In orchestrating both sides of the relationship, I never enjoy the depth another person will bring to the table.

Reflecting on the pieces

The first place I had to exercise that principle was in my marriage. Striking the balance between asserting myself, my thoughts and feelings and respecting the thoughts and feelings of another person could easily be described as the key element that brought my marriage to an end.

I had dated through most of high school and early college. There were a few long-term relationships and a few long-term crushes. All the while, I knew I felt different. By that I mean that the thoughts and experiences I was having didn't match up with what I was observing in others and what they seemed to be describing as their own experience of relationships. At the time I had no context to process it, let alone express it. I was also deeply entrenched in the process of perfecting the masks that both defined me and stole all self-definition from me. As I transitioned from college to adult life, dating fell to the back burner, although not for a lack of effort. There were those I pursued, some even rather intensely. I was living and working out of Nashville, Tennessee. Most of my time was spent traveling with various Christian musicians and my life on the road did not fare well with my social life.

Eventually I stepped out of the music business and started looking at going back to school and settling into full-time Christian ministry. The concept of "wife" and "family" fit quite well into that paradigm.

That's when I met M. She was a single mom attending my parents' church in East Tennessee. I started to get to know both M and her three-year-old daughter at events with the singles and career group at the church. We hung out at lunches after church, served together at outreach events and other church functions. If I were to try and describe the best way to get to know a potential life partner, there were a lot of things about our friendship that fit the model. We were friends first, and things grew from there. And when they started to grow, they grew fast.

We first discussed having a more serious relationship after the Fourth of July weekend in 1998. At the end of August, she took me to the airport to fly to a friend's wedding in Alaska. On the way down we stopped for lunch. Somewhere between talking about classes in the upcoming semester and the anticipation of my Alaskan adventure, I pulled a brochure out of my bag. It had diagrams of princess, square, rectangle, and oval cuts. It told about color and clarity. As I handed it to her, I confessed that heading to my friend's wedding had me thinking.

"If I were to get you a ring someday," I asked, "What would you like?"

By the first of October, I had designed a ring for her. I planned a romantic encounter underneath a tree in the back of my house. Unfortunately, the herd of cattle that shared my backyard became curious about the picnic basket I had left holding a bottle of wine. By the time we walked to the field, about 30 cows had taken over the spot. I suggested we walk up the hill a ways. Out of breath from the climb, but from a spot where we could see Tennessee, North Carolina, Virginia, and Kentucky, I asked her to be my wife.

From the time I left Nashville to the time we were married, less than 11 months had passed. Granted, I've heard stories of faster courtships resulting in highly successful, life-long marriages. Looking back there were some mitigating circumstances that should have raised concerns for both of us. But we were relatively young, ready to settle into our lives, and we truly loved each other.

Marriage math

Something I was told from a young age and didn't fully understand until about ten years into my own marriage — when I first started to peel back the masks and get honest with myself — is this simple truth: marriage strengthens whole people but it will never "fix" anyone. I often describe it this way: in marriage, $1 + 1 = 1$ and $\frac{1}{2} + \frac{1}{2} = 1/4$. It's only when two whole people, content in their own skin, come together, that a whole, healthy marriage might be expected. Wholeness shouldn't be confused with perfection. The concept of wholeness is a moving target and there are likely as many descriptions of what it looks like as there are people in the world. But having a grip on one's own sense of what it means to be whole without the addition of an intimate relationship is vital to the success and health of any marriage.

I came into our marriage knowing full well that I had struggles and baggage that I had not addressed in my life. Wholeness was a long way off. Everything from a solid vision for my career to my self-image and identity, to my personal and spiritual convictions (most of them masks), to my sexual comfort and security — all of it was in a state of flux and I couldn't see it, or at least wouldn't admit it.

One of the ways that I thought marriage was going to fix me was by fixing her, or more accurately "rescuing" her. I had ridden in on a white steed and had a reputation for storming in, taking no prisoners, and asking few questions. M was having intense issues with her family as well as the father of her daughter. Before all was said and done, I would physically put myself in harm's way in an effort to protect my young family.

Anyone I have ever talked to who is or has been married will always agree on at least two things: marriage will bring out the truth in all of us, and often will bring out the worst in all of us as well. Those who can survive this are the ones we see happily holding hands in the park after fifty, sixty or seventy years together. It's not that they are blissfully ignorant; it's that they are seasoned with the intimate ugliness of each other. They have chosen to find the great beauty in their partner in the middle of the loveable and the unlikeable.

Was it worth it?

My ugliness came to the surface and my perspective on God, truth, and life evolved. As my masks were removed, I changed. Eventually I had changed to a point that she no longer felt I was the person she married. She was right. While that's not something I apologize for — I never vowed not to change — it is something that saddens me. If I could do it again and be more genuine from day one, I would. In changing, I saw her in a different light. She was set in her ways and would work hard to bring others around her in line with thoughts, plans, and ideas. My penchant to change and her aversion to it became toxic. But as the great country crooner of the '90s, Garth Brooks, so eloquently sang, "I could have missed the pain. But I'd have had to miss the dance."

I would not want to have missed that dance. I have three amazing children. And years of memories and growing that never would have happened otherwise. It is, for better or worse, part of my journey that I am grateful to have taken. I've seen many people celebrating the day their divorces are finalized. Given their circumstances, I don't blame them. I was not one of those people. We handled the divorce ourselves; there were no attorneys involved. The day it was finalized it was just the judge, the bailiff, and me in the courtroom.

The galley was completely empty and the chamber had an eerie echo to it. Within a matter of five minutes the necessary questions had been asked, the paperwork reviewed, and the signatures confirmed.

The marriage was officially over.

Order for tomorrow

I don't know exactly what tomorrow holds on the relational front. But I'm learning to be patient. I'm learning to listen to both my head and my heart. I'm learning that I don't need to be fixed, I don't need to be needed and I don't need to fix anyone. I do need love. I do need respect. I do need to be desired.

I have had to come to terms with my fears for the future — specifically questioning what relationships are going to look like. After some intentional ambiguity as I began to transition — as

I said before, I was just climbing out of a box and I wasn't eager to throw myself into another one — I came to terms with the fact that I am a woman who is attracted to women. (It was February 7, 2015 — one of those blessing/curse things about being a chronic journaler.) There are still large, looming questions about my own desires and feelings to play out. This doesn't even take into consideration the complexities of a physical relationship. It all feels extremely complicated; who would willingly embrace this level of complexity in their lives if they had any other choice? How could I honestly and selflessly ask anyone to do so?

While I may not have chosen the complexity of my life, I have chosen the path toward wholeness and healing. That is something for which I have no desire to turn back the clock. Forward is the best and only option and the future is already so much brighter than the past. My greatest challenge as I work through this process and attempt to guard my own sanity is to simply "be." No gender — no sex — no social construct — to the extent possible, even no concern of physical self (*care* — but not *concern*). For right now, caring for myself mentally will come to the extent that I am able to exist at the level of my soul. I have already begun to rebuild from there, but it will take time, endurance, and a passion for the adventure of it.

The difference between being needed and desired, between manipulating a person in the guise of a relationship and loving them in absolute freedom, are pillars of my new concept of self. These are the concepts that have staying power.

Laura Beth Taylor

Chapter 10:

The Mask of Knowing

"It's a new day and I'm learning that questions are not necessarily doubts, and doubts are not evil. They are simply a stop on our journey toward wisdom."

For most of my life, if I had a thought that I saw as quote worthy, I arbitrarily attributed it to a mentor or an old friend. I was absolutely convinced that if anyone thought it was my own original idea, it would be dismissed and not taken seriously. That's changed. Maybe it's the natural wisdom that supposedly comes with age, or more likely it's that I've become much less concerned about what others think about me.

One such catchphrase that I attributed to a mentor was an adaptation of an old standard: It's not what you know or who you know; it's what you know *about* who you know. While that sounds like a recipe for blackmail, the point is actually quite the opposite. For relationships to really work, we need to actually know things about each other. I need to know your hobbies, your passions, the ages of your kids or grandkids, your profession, your hometown, and so on. When I know all these things, my interaction with you becomes much more relevant. I can ask you questions about things you actually have knowledge and enjoy talking about. I can connect with you on a deeper level and help you find others with similar passions. We can become a better, stronger extension of each other's network.

Old friends

For some people, knowing someone their whole lives is a common occurrence; a natural outcome of growing up in the same town where they were born. Maybe you grew up in the same house and next to the same group of kids since you were a child. You started school together, suffered through your teens, and managed to stay connected through transitions into college and careers. Our family's frequent moves made that rather difficult. Difficult, but not impossible. The longest friendship bond I've known is with our family friends, the Carlsons.

Our two families met when our dads were both stationed aboard a destroyer based out of San Diego, California. Bill and Dad had roomed together on a long cruise. Being that dad was a supply officer and Bill an engineer, the two were natural adversaries. Engineering never puts orders in properly and supply officers never have the right parts when they are needed. It's a vicious cycle. For some reason, their commanding officer decided it would help the situation if they were suitemates. The cruise was brutally long. They were both very eager and ready for time at home with their families. There was one little catch. During this long cruise, Moms and Joyce had become fast friends. The Carlsons had two boys roughly the same ages as Kayla and me. Dinners, picnics, and park outings were scheduled in black ink on our calendars. A friendship was going to be forged, even if out of fire.

Our families remained close over the years, even as we each jumped between duty stations. We enjoyed three-day weekend visits and summer camping trips in the Blue Ridge Mountains. At some point, the two moms and four kids piled into our Caprice (the replacement car from our collision several years earlier) and traveled west through Indiana to New Mexico. We completely wore out an 8-track tape of Neil Diamond's "The Jazz Singer" that summer, stopped at nearly every Dairy Queen between Virginia and New Mexico, and created incredible memories with each mile that passed.

The summer I turned 9 was set to be the greatest adventure of my young life. I flew *by myself* from the airport in Norfolk Virginia to Dulles International Airport, where Joyce and Bill picked me up for a two-week stay with their family. Going to bed the night before I left, I was a resolved and brave world traveler with my bags packed and ready. All my bravery dissolved when I woke up the next morning. The sky was packed with low, dark clouds dumping buckets of water and shouting at me with intense bursts of thunder and lightening.

"Are you ready to go?" Mom asked as I stared out the window at the chaos being unleashed just a thin pane of glass away. *Had I heard her right?*

"We can't fly in this weather!" I declared with marked disappointment.

"Oh, it's just a passing storm — it will be fine. Now head to the car."

Mom and Dad both accompanied me to my seat on the Allegheny Airlines Jet. We exchanged hugs and kisses and then they left. The flight attendant sealed the door tight behind them, sealing my fate in the process. This was how my short life was going to end, I was certain of it. Sitting right next to me, which I would learn later was no coincidence, was Admiral Taylor, one of dad's senior officers and a kind and gracious man. His presence was calming, but the rain continued to dance off the rounded window next to me and the ominous sky still taunted me as we pulled back from the gate. The occasional crack of thunder was off in the distance by this point, but it was close enough to reinforce my belief that that "up" was not the safest place we could go. My stomach pushed to the back of my body and my knuckles turned white as snow as the noisy engines hurled us down the runway. As we left the ground, it felt as if the nose of the plane pointed straight up, like a Blue Angel at an airshow. As quickly as it could, the jet carried us up until the clouds swallowed us, and for what seemed like an eternity, the turbulent air knocked us around.

Then something amazing happened: we broke through the top of the clouds and were greeted by bright blue skies and a big golden sun. The clouds that had been thick and dark when I was beneath them floated below me like puffy white sheets of cotton; not even the least bit threatening. The plane leveled out and the short hop to Washington passed by without incident. Even still, I breathed a sigh of relief and the color finally returned to my fingers when the seal on that door was broken and I was escorted off the airplane and up the ramp. I was recalling this event in a recent conversation with Joyce and she reminded me of Admiral Taylor's loud reminder as we emerged into the terminal: "Remember what your mom said about changing your underwear everyday."

Despite the embarrassment, perhaps in light of it, I was relieved to see familiar faces when Joyce and the boys greeted me at the gate that day. For the next two weeks, I was a third son to them and the summer adventures completely lived up to my high expectations.

Incidentally, I learned to love flying, even chalking up about sixty hours in a small Cessna 172 when working for a flight school in the early 2000s. It's still on my bucket list to earn a private pilot's license.

My junior year of high school, I was selected to once again go to Washington, D.C. for a statewide Christian youth leadership conference. I have two memories of that event:

1) Walking on the senate floor and sitting in
Virginia Senator Paul Treble's seat. (It was an
incredible chamber of history and influence, regardless
of your political views.)

2) Returning to our hotel room from that Capital
visit to be welcomed by a crab cake Joyce delivered for
my birthday. No, not a cake baked with crustaceans,
but a birthday cake shaped like a crab; complete with
red icing. To this day, no one really remembers the
inspiration for the cake, but the result created a lasting
impression, one neither she nor I have let the other
live down.

Eventually, Moms, Dad, Joyce, and Bill retired to
two 5-acre plots right next to each other on a
Tennessee ridgetop. Joyce and Bill continue to serve as
parental figures to me to this day, and are known as
Grandma Joyce and Grandpa Bill to my kids. They are
familiar, comfortable fixtures in my life. When I see an
old Victrola, I make a mental note to ask Bill about

that particular model. When I see a Department 56 ceramic house, I wonder if Joyce has that edition. Without a doubt when I see a bright red crab on a Christmas ornament or a birthday card, I scoop it up to remind Joyce of our great memories together. I know them and they know me, and I love them for their constant presence in my life.

New friends

When 2014 ushered in this transitional stage of my life, affirming my identity and asking tough questions about my faith meant that I was stepping away from social and professional networks I'd been building for years. While a handful of people have stuck with me through the journey, many chose to step away. It had been a decade and a half since I pursued friendships and social interaction as an individual, rather than as a couple. Still working with me through symptoms of depression and anxiety, my therapist strongly advised I find a support group. It didn't really matter to her *what* they were supporting — gender identity, codependency, progressive Christianity — her exact words were "pick one of the things you're dealing with, and find people to be around who understand."

Of all the challenges I was facing, the most daunting at that moment was the separation and pending divorce with M. After some fancy Google work, I found a group that met in a church in Dallas. It was perfect. It was outside of my old community so I was not likely to run into people I already knew. Although they met in a church, they were not specifically a religious group. I needed room for my faith to breath and a group where I wasn't pressured to believe one way or another would allow that space.

It didn't take long before I realized that the real strength of the group was the social interaction outside of the weekly meeting. When those Friday and Saturday evenings that used to be reserved for time with a spouse rolled around, I now had options.

Feeling an ever-increasing freedom to be me, the Saturday before I first introduced myself to the group as Laura Beth, I joined in a crowd of us gathering at a Mexican café south of Dallas for an evening of margaritas and karaoke. Before I knew it, I was standing there with a microphone in hand crooning to Billy Joel's "Piano Man." Naturally, I adjusted the lyrics to reflect a "Piano Person" and to ask "John at the bar" why he called me "Bill."

That night, I stepped back into the role of entertainer (not an unintentional reference to another Joel classic) — a persona I had long since abandoned under pressure to be so many other things to so many other people. The faces sitting at those tables had smiles on them as I sang and, just as important to me, friends and strangers alike laughed at my antics. It was a moment of great renewal and hope for all that lay ahead. It was through friendships forged in the circle that I gathered with each Tuesday night that I was encouraged to start blogging, to write this book, and to reengage with life. They didn't accept me as a transgender woman; they just accepted *me*.

As I reengaged, I started to step out of that circle into the big, wide world that awaited me. The first time I walked into a room filled with predominantly Christian women was when I attended a seminar being presented by Rachel Held Evans. I had recently read her first book, *Faith Unraveled*. It not only captured my attention because it addressed so many of the questions I was asking both God and myself at the time, but also because much of the story took place in Rachel's hometown of Dayton, Tennessee. This also happens to be the adopted hometown of all my extended family. I have been visiting my sister and eventually my parents there for nearly 25 years. I recognized the landmarks and even knew some of the people she referenced in the book. It was familiar, and I was excited to have the opportunity to hear and meet her in person.

Then I walked into the room. I quickly realized that, despite resonating with Rachel's writing, there was no guarantee that the people in the room were going to accept me as I am — a transgender woman still fairly early in my transition. Letting that awareness sink in, I took a deep breath and moved forward to find a seat. In a denim skirt, red blouse and blue heels, I strolled up the aisle and found a seat about four rows from the front. Rachel was giving two lectures that morning, and prior to the first I sat as still as possible, hoping to blend in much as I could. Every detail of how I sat and moved, how I touched my hair, or folded my hands was painfully on my mind.

At the end of the first lecture, there was time for questions and discussion. I don't remember what the statement was or why it bothered me, but a larger man with thick dark hair about six rows behind me said something that didn't set well in my spirit. So I replied. About halfway through my opening sentence, as I felt every pair of eyes in the room staring holes into my very soul, something occurred to me: *speaking up was not the best way to blend in.* I once again breathed through the moment, made my point, and the conversation carried on. There were no shouts of objection, no confrontations from incensed, pious church people and no villagers with torches and pitchforks breaking down the doors. Instead, my comments were met with nods of agreement. Perhaps this *was* all going to work out after all!

After the second workshop I introduced myself to Rachel and made the connection to my family in Tennessee. A month later I was visiting Dayton and she agreed to meet me for a cup of coffee, which quickly turned to soft serve yogurt when we realized the coffee shop was closed for the day. Listening compassionately to my story, she guided me toward organizations like The Reformation Project and the Gay Christian Network. She pointed out conferences I needed to attend and blogs I needed to follow. In short — she jump-started my new social network.

Sitting behind me that day at the workshop was Dr. Jackie Roese, a pastor, teacher, and writer whom I had worked with in past ministry experiences. She didn't recognize me, which was actually a relief, but she did embrace me. Through a subsequent email exchange, she introduced me to a friend of hers at a church called Serenity. From there, I found my new church home.

Breathing through the anxiety, stepping past the fears, I once again started to know people and, as a welcome change, began to be known for who I really am. That was, and is still, a liberating experience.

Knowing God

"Deconstruction" is a major buzzword among those questioning their childhood faith. I've read it. I've heard it. I've used it. There are plenty of volumes, articles, and essays that address the idea, what it is, and how to accomplish it.

Deconstructing my own faith is leading to a personal revival in my heart and mind. As I became willing to be led by God through a new journey of discovery, I learned that there is no hurry. I was brought up with a sense of intellectual urgency as it pertained to my faith and being able to articulate it. Without a doubt, we need to be reasonable and accountable in what we practice and teach others. However, that does not translate into having all the answers all the time. In fact, when I allowed for the reality that I would always have more questions than answers, and that perhaps God had even *designed* it that way, my faith became more free to accept, and my mind more free for the pursuit of wisdom in favor of knowledge.

I began to find tidbits of truth spread throughout the world. In science, in ancient texts of wisdom, in meditation, and in creation itself. Revelations began to emerge. I came to be utterly convinced that all truth is God's truth, and while I still believe that all Scripture is true (when properly understood in the context of language and culture), not all truth is in Scripture.

The process of finding that freedom has led to a baseline for deconstruction. It's the bedrock foundation that I have found to hold the rest of my belief about God, who God is and how God relates to me. It comes back to a simple statement: God is either sovereign or not.

There will never be a scientific solution to that proposition. It's one each sojourner must be willing to step toward in faith. Having taken the step to accept God's sovereignty, I have found the rest of the questions I ask take on a different hue. They are either seen through the shade of a God who exists and is engaged, or does not and isn't. Other pursuits, my study of psychology for example, are then opened both to the sovereignty of God and the understanding of humankind, without conflict. My study of Scripture can be informed equally by history and by general revelation.

Even accepting God's sovereign nature however, I still resonate with a question that permeates most lines of deconstructionist thinking: Is God someone we can know?

My response to that would have surprised the Bible student wearing my skin 25 years ago: "No, God is too abstract and too complex." Doubts about God's nature and behavior (if we can even call it that) are not exceptional; they are a natural part of the quest. But that doesn't mean *seeking* to know God is not worth the journey.

Unlike people we get to know in our webs of social networking or lifelong experience, knowing God is a mysterious undertaking. God is infinite and we are finite. God is supernatural and we are natural. God is eternal — always was, always will be, existing outside the confines of time — and we are temporal, locked into the progressive path through seconds, hours, days, and years. After years of being warned not to be "so open-minded that my brains leaked out," I arrived at the conclusion that my mind, and the empirical knowledge it collects, is of very little use when it comes to truly knowing God. It is only *one* of my tools on the journey, and perhaps not even the *best* tool.

I breathed a sigh of relief when I finally let myself rest in the fact that knowing God had little to do with actual knowledge — there would be no multiple choice or short answer questions on a final exam — but everything to do with pursuit. Not a moment of growth in my life has come from having knowledge, but rather from the process of attempting to acquire it and the love I invest in relationships along the way. The joy is truly in the journey.

The biggest mask yet

Shedding the need to know, and recovering from an addiction to answers, has been the hardest of my masks to shatter. There is a false sense of security in knowledge; a myth that we connect to the world around us through answers to specific questions. While it may be beneficial to know what we know about who we know, the ultimate power of relationships is unlocked when we combine knowledge with sincere love, compassion, and empathy. We can lull ourselves to sleep at night with the belief that all is in order simply because we are convinced we can explain it. That doesn't mean that it is in order or that our explanations are accurate.

Science is less about *proving* and more about *understanding* reality within the confines of nature. Faith, on the other hand is less about limiting possibilities and allowing God to be big, allowing for the *super* natural. I had been taught that Jesus came to fill a God-shaped hole in my heart but in the process of trying to fill that hole, I created a God-shaped box in my head.

It finally hit me, what I had been saying for years was true: it's not what we know or who we know: old friends, new friends, God or even myself; it's what we know about who we know — the experiences we have with one another — that truly enriches our lives. The mask finally came crumbling down when I let God out of the box. I realized I could drift off to sleep with no need to explain God, humanity, or the universe.

I rest in the freedom of being me, and I feel joyful in believing God takes pleasure in me, having created me in God's image and embracing me as God's own child.

Shattering Masks

Bonus Section:

The Defensive Nature of Being Offended

Of all the posts that I have put on the blog since I started it, this is perhaps my favorite series. It's also one to which I think individuals on both sides of any debate need to pay attention. It is still available on the blog, but I'm hoping it may get into even more hands — and minds — by including it here as well.

Introduction

"I find you offensive." It was only the third time since beginning my transition that a random stranger had approached me with any sort of criticism. The first was a well-intentioned older lady in a Starbucks who informed me I was an abomination (she abandoned the conversation after she couldn't give me chapter and verse — I gave it to her instead). The second, also in a Starbucks, was a couple of smart aleck teenage boys who were no doubt still in search of their own identities. This third encounter was with another older lady, this time in a McDonald's (I opted for a dollar coke instead of a $4 coffee — the joys of a starving writer and student).

I had my headphones on and was reading a book on my iPad. I hadn't noticed her approach me, but she spoke loud enough for me to hear her over Journey. (Seriously — who interrupts Journey?)

I took my ears out and looked up at her, "Excuse me?"

She stood her ground and repeated her position, "I find you offensive."

"Oh," I said after a brief moment of stunned and confused silence. "Well," I continued, "I find you defensive."

She looked at me like I had slapped her.

"What does that mean?"

"I don't know. I'll have to think through it. But I definitely find you defensive."

I truly didn't know exactly what I meant. I was rather hoping she would sit down and we could have a friendly dialogue on the subject, perhaps bridging some generation gaps. She had other things to do apparently. The party she had been waiting on appeared from the restroom and she was off without another word.

I don't know if I was subconsciously being fed by the Sunday afternoon sports analysis murmuring from the TV on the walls in the background or if there was something from my past that bubbled up in that moment, but I had a hard time thinking about much of anything else for a while. I've never been one to shy away from sports — I lettered in high school — but I've never really been given to team sports analogies. Why did I find her defensive? What might she have been defending? Was I being offensive? What is the difference between offense and defense? I don't often get offended, why is that?

Game on.

The offensive side of defense

Anyone who has worked in the church for any length of time will likely all be able to agree on one thing: you are going to offend someone. For that matter, anyone who has managed people, worked with people, walked down the same sidewalk with another person, has likely had the experience of offending someone, being offended or both.

But what does the anatomy of an offense look like? I wanted to break it down and try and understand what is really going on in someone's mind when they have the feeling of being offended. Following is my observation, and to help explain it, I turn to the turf of Texas, the good ole gridiron, the pigskin playground: American Football.

Just to make sure we are all on the same page, I'll start with some football basics (for those who may need a little "101" course): The objective of the game is for the team who has possession of the ball, referred to as the "offense," to advance the ball down the field and into the "end zone" thus scoring a "touchdown" (queue the awkward celebration dance). This would be easy except for the fact that the team who does not have possession of the ball, referred to as the "defense" is doing everything they can to stop this advance. It is on this conflict that the entire interest in the game is based.

Each time the advance of the offense is stopped by the defense the ball is placed at that spot, which then becomes known as "the line of scrimmage." The teams line up, the ball is put into motion and the offensive assault resumes.

Suppose for a moment that when the ball goes into motion, instead of trying to advance the ball, the offense just passively stands there holding it. They make no attempt to cross the line into the opposition's territory. The defense, however, crosses the line and aggressively pursues the ball on the side of the line where the offense lined up. They are now the aggressor — the defense has gone on the offensive. The offense, on the other hand, now finds themselves in the position of defending the territory of the field that was already theirs. The offense now has to be defensive.

As I thought through my encounter in McDonald's, specifically my gut reaction that my critic was acting defensively, it made me realize that when we are "offended" by something, we are often playing the side of the defense against an offense that is standing still — making no real attempt to advance against us. The advance that we feel is a perceived advance, which prompts us to become defensive. Rather than defending our own position, we are much more comfortable going on the offense and attacking the person or idea we find "offensive" and forcing them into the position of having to defend their position instead.

The next question then is "What is it that we believe requires defending?" In the case of my would-be friend at McD's, I can only hypothesize as to what she might have said if we could have had that conversation. Perhaps she was defending her interpretation of a religious standard, maybe she saw me as an assault on cultural norms, she could have thought I was invading her space as a feminist, it could have even been that I smelled like I live on a boat and this had nothing to do with gender at all. The point is that as a defensive player she did not do a very good job of protecting her territory; I don't have a clue what territory she was trying to defend.

Here is the takeaway (the interception, the recovered fumble — just to drive the analogy into the ground): When you find yourself offended, know what it is that you are defending and be ready to mount a proper defense before you step on the field.

(And for the record — I do have a nice shower on the boat. I smell fine, I promise.)

Fielding a good defense

Despite my people-pleasing tendencies, I've never been one to shy away from a conflict (except with those I'm very close to, but that's for another discussion). I respect a good debate. I'm impressed with someone who can articulate his position in a diplomatic, well-thought manner — even if I don't agree with him.

What I don't like is when conflict and disagreement devolve into personal attacks and needless digs. I also don't like being in conflict with an opposition that is not willing to listen or have genuine dialogue. I confess that at times I have been guilty of all those things — we all have our moments. But as a whole, I strive for productive encounters when conflict exists.

To that end, I have some suggestions for anyone who might find me offensive. I realize of course that if you find me offensive, you are highly unlikely to be reading this, but translate this to apply to any moment where you may feel offended by something or someone.

1) Recognize that you are actually on the defense. Be honest with yourself about what you are defending.

2) Set a goal for your defense. Do you need to make a point to me? Do you need to make a point to people around us or to society in general? Do you simply need closure personally? All of these are valid, but will change the way you approach the subject.

3) Organize your thoughts. Be ready to explain your thoughts and feelings on the subject — keeping a clear distinction between what you believe are facts and what are clearly your opinions.

Again, both have a place in the conversation, but keeping them separate will go a long way toward building and maintaining your credibility.

4) Be as ready to listen as you are to speak. Much of the offense we feel in life may be easily reframed when we allow for a correction of our perception by understanding the intention of the other party.

5) If all above fails and you still need to talk — just ask me questions. I'm such a sucker for a good conversation I will very likely hand you all the information you need to make a case against me. And, if I'm taking my own advice, I'll probably ask you questions that will clarify why you were offended in the first place!

There is a quote most often attributed to Winston Churchill that says diplomacy is simply the art of "telling someone to go to hell and still getting them excited about the trip." A little thought, intentionality, and diplomacy go a long way in managing your feeling of being offended.

If you found any of this offensive, please feel free to practice in the comments below.

Drawing lines

In 1771, a group of Bostonians dressed up as Native Americans, boarded some British cargo ships and threw all the tea overboard. Why? Boundaries. They had drawn the line at taxation without representation.

In 1962, President Kennedy sent warships to blockade the route to Cuba. Why? Boundaries. The United States drew the line at arming communist Cuba with Russian missiles. (The crisis was also provoked by the fact that Fidel Castro felt violated when the U.S. attempted to break his boundaries with the failed Bay of Pigs invasion.)

About 10 minutes ago I watched a four-year-old boy clock his slightly older sister in the cheek. Why? You guessed it — boundaries. Apparently he had drawn the imaginary line and he was taking retribution for her being "on his side" of the booth where they sat waiting for their dad to return with happy meals. Dad was unaware of the developments and I imagined big sister quietly plotting her revenge (no wait, that wasn't imagination, it was a flashback).

Keep looking though history, scriptures (of any faith), classroom rules, self-help books, you name it, and you will see that boundaries are everywhere. Everywhere, that is, except in the life of a people pleaser who had always prided herself in "never really being offended by anything." Come to find out I was never offended by anything because there was never a line to cross. I knew what "sin" looked like, that is I knew when you or I were crossing lines that I believed God had drawn. I had boundaries for other people; I would go in guns ablaze when I thought someone else's boundaries were being violated.

So draw the line at drawing lines for myself? Why have I held so tightly to the notion that there is something inherently bad in setting my own boundaries? I have come up with a list.

1) The prevailing cultural myth that boundaries are selfish. As a culture we have a twisted view of what is "selfish." Let me see if I can sum it up: anything you do that is more about you than it is about me is selfish. In essence, I will define your selfishness by my own selfishness with the implicit understanding that yours is much, much worse than mine.

In the last year I've been learning the difference between being self-centered and self-caring: "self-centered" means that I am focused inward on me at the exclusion of you (we can't have two centers), "self-caring" means that I will focus on you while maintaining a healthy awareness of my own physical, emotional, and spiritual needs. How can I do that? Boundaries.

2) The core belief that I don't deserve boundaries. Very closely related to and perhaps perpetuated by the myth in the first point is the core belief that I don't deserve to draw any lines that will in some way give even the perception that I have placed my needs, wants, or desires over someone else's. I haven't really ventured too deeply into the source of this belief. I've been toying with a bunch of notions including a fixation on my failures, symptoms of PTSD, and a lack of strong identity.

Regardless of the source, the only thing that I have found to counter the distortion that I deserve less than all others in my life: boundaries.

3) The illusion of servanthood. I say the "illusion" of servanthood because I'm trying to make a distinction between moments when my heart is in the right place and those when I am trying to live up to a perceived expectation. It's really as simple as being honest with myself about why I do the things I do. Am I motivated by fear or friendship; compassion or compulsion; affection or addiction?

The best way I have learned to keep myself on track: boundaries.

4) The missing emotional vocabulary. Knowing what to say and when to say it is something at which I usually excel in business, teaching, or even casual social engagements. I do just fine as long as you don't ask me to engage my feelings. When an emotion swells up — positive or negative, it doesn't matter — spoken words often fail me. Maintaining boundaries requires us to be able to articulate those boundaries in both practical and emotional terms. Sometimes that is as simple as knowing when to say "no," other times it means being prepared to explain why you hold to some of your core values and morals. Historically, I would rather forego the boundary than take the leap and vocalize what that knot in my stomach is trying to say.

The best way I have found to expand my emotional vocabulary: well actually therapy and healthy friendships (both maintained by: boundaries).

Conclusion

So there it is: what it meant that I found my would-be accuser "defensive." That whole encounter took less that 20 seconds, but sparked a wonderful opportunity to explore some things that had been bubbling in my brain. I come back to this McDonald's on a somewhat regular basis. I've yet to see my offended friend again, but when I do, I hope she has more time to talk. I think I'm ready now!

Resources: When I was first wrestling with issues of faith, gender and sexuality, I desperately needed places I could go to learn more and talk with others on a similar journey. Below are two websites of organizations I found most helpful and highly respect. Also if you are a parent of an LGBT child, reach out to me on the blog and I can connect you with some wonderful people to walk this journey with you.

1. www.thereformationproject.com - The Reformation Project was founded by Matthew Vines, author of *God and the Gay Christian*, to help educate Christians in affirming interpretations of scripture.

2. www.gaychristian.net - The Gay Christian Network (GCN) was founded by Justin Lee to promote a greater sense of community among LGBT Christians.

3. www.sophiasojourn.com - Once again, this is my blog. There are many resources out there included other bloggers, a bibliography and discussions related to specific scripture.

For information on booking for speaking engagements or other appearances, please contact me at **laurabeth@sophiasojourn.com** or visit the blog at **www.sophiasojourn.com**.

The following is approved for reproduction in promotional material:

Laura Bethany Taylor is a blogger and advocate for marginalized people in faith communities. She has a degree in Communications and Christian Ministry from Dallas Baptist University and over 25 years of experience in various ministry platforms. Laura Beth organized Sophia Sojourn as a not-for-profit corporation to serve as a platform for helping others understand and tell their own and to work with churches and other entities to help them move toward greater experiences of compassion and inclusion. She currently lives in North Texas near her three kids and granddaughter, but enjoys traveling throughout the country.